MW00763384

1

I REMEMBER

By D. W. Reavis

"I remember the days
of old." Psalms 143:5

**REVIEW AND HEARLD PUBLISHING ASSOCIATION
TAKOMA PARK, ASHINGTON, D. C.**

PRINTED IN THE U.S.A.

Copyright 2014, by Gerald E. Greene
All rights reserved

ISBN 978-1500388898

This is a reprint of an edition with no publication date using a modern font. Some spellings have been updated to reflect current usage.

In spite of his naivety regarding the feelings and opinions of slaves, I found this book to have significant value regarding the history of the Seventh-day Adventist church and Battle Creek College.

Gerald E. Greene
geraldegreene@gmail.com

CONTENTS

I Remember

FOREWORD

UPON the often-repeated requests of many of my intimate friends to whom I have related some of my experiences, I venture to publish some of them, not because I regard them as unusual and worthy of publication, but simply to comply with the wishes of my friends—a natural characteristic of my eighty -one years of life—an inborn weakness, some may say; but to me the pleasing of my friends has been a source of great happiness all through my life.

To reveal frankly my age at the very beginning of my story is to confess my entrance into second childhood. Children under eight years of age consider it important to stress their age upon the slightest provocation; but after they attain the age of sixteen, they are usually reluctant to reveal their age, especially girls, until they reach the sixties or seventies, when the age-telling incentive comes back to all except spinsters, who seem possessed with a hallucination that all will think them younger than they are, if their exact age is not known.

All through my life I have had no birthday celebrations or reminders of my birth of any kind. When I was a child, there were other things of greater importance for my parents and guardians to think of. When I grew up, I did not have the birthday habit, and I thought nothing about it, nor about how old I was. Sometimes I would actually forget just how old I was, and would have to refer to the record in the old family Bible to refresh my memory on this unimportant matter. In time, through observation, I reached the conclusion that almost all adults overemphasize their age—that if they would forget their age, they would remain young longer. I believe that scripture which assures us that as a man "thinketh in his heart, so is he." If he things he is old and keeps that in his mind, his body will gradually come into harmony with his mind, and he will be old quicker than if he did not think about it.

Until I was eighty I thought so little of my age I would always have to figure from my birth year (1853), which I never forgot, before I could tell my exact age. Of course, I always knew within a few years, but the exact number of years I could not tell. I was not at all like the good seventy-year old brother I recently met on the street, hobbling along on his cane, who in prompt reply to my inquiry as to how he was getting along, said: "Tolerably well, for a man seventy years of age, if I live until the fifteenth of next month." Nor was I like another sixty-year-old brother who came stumblingly along as I was painting the roof of my house, and was greatly alarmed because I was on the roof. He commanded me to come right down, and expressed surprise that a man of my age did not know better than to expose myself to such danger, and admonished me to remember I was *an old man*. I told him I did not allow the thought of being old to shackle me in any work needing to be done, as he evidently did. Even today, were I not forced by my friends to think of it, I would, judging from the way I feel and the ability I have to get around, guess I was about as old as most men are at fifty.

I have always been proud of the fact that I was born and reared to the mature years of twenty-one on the rich prairies of the State of Missouri as it was in its early days—the "Show Me" State. Many uninformed people suppress a smile when I announce the place of my nativity, because they believe that fabricated story of the State being called the "Show Me" State, on account of its native people being so dull it was necessary to demonstrate, to prove every new idea to them. The early settlers of Missouri were of the purest American stock, hard-working, honest men and women, but they were so imposed upon by those coming from other States and other countries that they became suspicious of all strangers, and demanded proof of good faith in all business transactions. Hence the State was dubbed the "Show me." State. It was the one State of the Union in which its native-born people demanded a clear record of all newcomers before they accepted them—a State of aristocratic slave owners, especially in all that part of the State south of Mason and Dixon's line, in which section I grew up.

The Missouri Homestead

MY OLD PLANTATION HOME

MY MEMORY reaches back to a few years before the Civil War. Previous to that time, my information comes from near relatives, who often repeated to me things I was too young to know about in any other way. My father and his father were slaveholders in that part of Missouri permitting slavery. I was told that our family were descendants of one Ashley Reavis, who came over to this country with the Jamestown, Virginia, settlement. His name was Ashley when he came over, but he married a lady by the name of Reavis, and took her name, which seemed at that time to be admissible in a case where the woman was a property owner and her family better known that that of the man. This branch of the Reavis family were inclined to frontier life. They kept close to the frontier as the country developed westward.

Long before I came upon the stage of action, my father secured a large tract of government land in western Missouri, for which he paid $1.25 an acre. There were few white people, no railroads, no telegraph wires, nothing but broad prairies and howling wolves. Kansas City was a mere village out on the western border of the State.

When he left the home plantation in Boonville, Missouri, his father gave him a horse, a saddle and a bridle, and a young Negro man, born on his own birthday. The young slave was worth, according to slave prices at that time, about $500. My father struck out with these possessions into the most unsettled part of the State—away from the Missouri River, along which the people usually settled, on account of its being the only way of travel excepting by ox or mule team and wagon.

Arrived at his destination, he built a log hut near a prairie stream, which was skirted by timber, and began to develop a plantation for himself. He put up a horsepower sawmill, a wool and cotton carding mill, and a corn gristmill operated on the old tread wheel power plan; also he put in a tannery, a wagon shop, blacksmith and carpenter shops, in all of which building he and Charles, his first Negro slave, were the only master mechanics.

When the Civil War came, my father had a prosperous plantation. There was a large frame and log residence, a huge barn, a carding mill, a smokehouse, a sawmill, a number of Negro cabins, and a few other small houses occupied by white people, who worked on the plantation as overseers. My father's large frame and log residence served also as the village tavern and stagecoach station.

He erected a frame store building near the house, and offered to give it to any one who would put in a stock of general merchandise. A young man by the name of Jack Lee accepted the offer, and put in the required stock, whereupon my father named the place "Leesville," which is even today a small country village. This village at the time of my childhood had about 200 inhabitants; so a schoolhouse was built upon our plantation, and a private school established. Also, a church was built halfway between Leesville and another plantation several miles away. All around the village were the fields of my father's plantation, and his various mills, factories, and other buildings.

Everything we used, with the exception of chinaware, glassware, pins, needles, and buttons, was raised or manufactured on our plantation. From raw wool, cotton, or fiber came our clothing. Slaves working under white bosses were skillful mechanics, and produced agricultural implements, wagons, buggies, and all kinds of tools. The few things we could not produce came by ox wagons from St. Louis, but there were no such things as silks, satins, ribbons, fancy buttons, and store shoes in those days. Yet they were days of abundance of the simple necessities of life, and of real satisfaction—days of physical and moral development, when a spirit of happiness and contentment prevailed.

The tannery, the shoe and leather factory, was some distance from the village, down by Tebo Creek, where water could be had in abundance for tanning purposes. All shoes for the family were made at the tannery. It was a great day for us children when in the late fall the old colored tanner and shoemaker took measurements for winter shoes. (In the summer we went barefooted.) From that day to the thrilling hour the shoes were brought to the "the big house" by the same dignified, serious tanner, every hour was one of enjoyable anticipation. A child of the present day would find no pleasure in the shoes that gave us as children such great delight, for they were made of heavy cowhide., on straight lasts, and pegged with heavy, homemade pegs. The soles were heavy, and they had large, low heels. But the squeak of our humble "new shoes" was music in our ears. In fact, squeaky shoes were *especially preferred*, because the squeak was a sure indication of newness. How proud and how pleased we were.

In those days, children, both white and black, had very limited clothing of any kind. I distinctly remember the one slip, made of homespun flax, which reached to about half-way between my

13

hips and my knees, as the only wearing apparel I had the year round, excepting home-knitted socks added in winter. When I grew so large I could not get into this slip, then it was given to a younger child, and I got another slip, which had been worn for several years by my older brother. These flax slips were usually washed by the Negroes after we children had retired, and were all dry and ironed and ready for us early in the morning. Children had no changes in clothing as they now have, excepting in rare instances where there were Sunday clothes, which were usually not much better than those worn during the week.

Children, both white and black, were put to work at a very early age. They had all the recreation it was thought they really needed in the easy work assigned them. They were taught to find pleasure and recreation in the work they were doing. To illustrate: When I followed the one-horse shovel plow during the time of the first plowing of corn, when it was very small, and uncovered that which the plow had nearly buried, I was told by a wise old Negro, who was doing the plowing, to play that the covered corn plants were people who were caught in a landslide, and that I was a rescuing party following in a wake of a great storm, sent to save the lives of the "corn people." In my childish imagination the thing was made real by the way the old man pictured it out to me. I worked in a frame of mind that obliterated time, and with zeal that produced health, and gave me physical, mental, and moral exercise.

One bright spot in my early memory was the thrilling twilight hours which we white children spent in the cabins of the slaves, enjoying the stories and the singing that always went on there. We usually stayed until the old house "mammy," upon the request of the "mist'ess," our mother, called, demanding our presence at "the big house." Only those who have had a similar experience can imagine the relish of such evenings. And our hosts apparently enjoyed us as audience, for often they joined us in pleading for an extension of our stay.

These associations of the white children and the colored people had their good and bad effects. They were good in that the colored people, as far as they knew, were strict in their application of principles, especially in the matter of discipline. Obedience—immediate obedience—to the known will of parents or to those in authority, was absolutely imperative. There were no "ifs" or "ands" about it. It was a law! And somehow their convictions were so strong on this point, and their looks and words and general demeanor were such in the presence of these requirements, that they forced unquestioning and immediate compliance on our part. They were good also in that the Negroes were naturally religiously inclined. They believed in an exacting, yet merciful God in a simple, confiding way that begot confidence in all who came in touch with them.

But these contacts were bad in that the Negroes were superstitious. They believed in a grotesque devil, and that he frequently appeared in all of the very worst forms imaginable. They believed also in the existence of ghosts and witches. Never can I forget the vivid impression made upon me when I was told, in a most hair-raising way, that every night after twelve o'clock the devil came and sat on top of the large gatepost at the entrance of the plantation yard, watching for all bad people; that he had a great head of iron, with horns, and fire in his mouth and eyes, and a great long tail, with a spear point; that in the blackness of night, ghosts and evil spirits abounded everywhere.

As a consequence I became afraid of night. I would never think of such a thing as going out by the big gate in front of the plantation after dark, even in company with other children. When I went out of that large gate with my parents at night, I was very careful to cling close to them for safety. For years I was a night coward and a day dreamer of spirits and ghosts. The colored people joyed in telling the most thrilling, goose-flesh-producing stories of ghosts it was possible for the human mind to invent.

Some distance from our community there was a stretch of wild prairie, miles long, lying between two reaches of highlands several miles apart. This place was known by colored people as "Spirit Valley," and many were the ghost stories associated with it. There was a wagon road or trail through this valley, but it was seldom traveled by the Negroes. It was the only road, how-ever, leading from our plantation to the flour mill, to which our wheat was taken twice a year to be ground and bolted into flour. It was always planned to make a daylight trip through this valley, but on one occasion, one of the wagons broke down en route, and night came on before repairs could be made. There those frightened black drivers were, stranded in the heart of "Spirit Valley," with "Devil's Ridge" on one side and "Indian Ridge" on the other, and on the very spot where it was said that fifteen or twenty families had been massacred by Indians in ear-lier days, "a long, long time ago."

There was no sleeping in the Negro cabins at the plantation that night at the usual bedtime, for all the colored people knew the mill teams must pass through "Spirit Valley" after Dark, seeing they had not arrived home earlier in the evening. There-fore, all the cabin tallow dips were alight when the wagons finally drove in, and subdued inquiries were made of the almost speechless and frightened travelers. Soon all the servants came together in one cabin to hear their stories. With the morning light, however, the spirits seemed to fade before cold reality, and the excitement died down.

At the breakfast table, my father heard some of their stories from us children and old Ann as she served, and he said the black boys saw only the images of their own imagination, and that the welts he found on the oxen were made by their whips in urging them through the valley, and not by spirits at all!

I Remember

THE FIDELITY OF THE OLD-TIME NEGRO SLAVE

THE old-time Negro was not "a hireling," according to the Saviour's definition of such a person in John 10:12, 13. The Negroes were usually zealous in protection and defense of their master's property. In fact, they regarded everything on the plantation as their own, and treated it accordingly. They did not trespass upon the property of others, and it was their ambition to apprehend trespassers. As an illustration of this old-time slave characteristic, the following instance may be selected from many others I could relate:

One hot summer evening, after it was quite dark, old Freem was returning from a neighboring plantation; and as he was passing one of my father's fields of corn, then in the roasting ear, he heard the familiar sound produced by breaking off ears, apparently a short distance from the fence. He saw where some of the top rails of the fence had been thrown off, so he made up his mind that some "low-down" person was stealing "Mass's" corn.

Being sure the robber would come out of the field where he had evidently entered, he crouched in the shadow of the lowered fence, and waited for the thief to appear. He did not have long to wait, for the intruder seemed to be in a great hurry, and came swiftly to the gap in the fence, with his arms full of roasting ears.

As he let them fall over the fence, some of them descended on Freem's head, and produced in him a still greater desire to punish the trespasser thoroughly. Then the robber began to climb clumsily over the fence. Just as soon as his feet touched the ground on the outside of the fence, Freem sprang up from behind him and grabbed him! Horror of horrors! Instantly the thief, a big black bear, sent forth a piercing guttural scream, and Freem matched it in volume of fright as he roared, "Lawsy me! A b'ar!" Both were so surprised and thoroughly frightened that the bear ran as fast as he could in one direction and Freem in the other—Freem toward the plantation and the bear toward the woods one-half mile away. Freem did not stop running nor attempt to look back until he rushed into the midst of a group of Negroes at his cabin door, and he was still so frightened that all he could say was, "Run! Run! De b'ar am a-cumin' !" Soon all the slave families were safely housed in their cabins with their doors barred. But the bear by that time was far, far away, in the rough timberland. Thereafter even the mention of the word "bear" would cause Freem to shudder.

The Christmas holiday week was a great time for Negroes in our part of Missouri. It was customary among plantation owners there to give their servants Christmas week off, requiring them during that time to do only the usual routine work, and that was planned to be as light as possible. For weeks before Christmas everything was in preparation for festal times. Feed for the stock, which was usually brought form the fields as needed, was hauled up and stored near the barns, in order that less time might be required in doing the feeding. Great piles of wood cut for the fireplaces and the cook stoves, were special holiday signs; new dresses—plain, but new—were in evidence; new shoes, new everything, indicated a time of great rejoicing and reveling in unpretentious happiness.

During Christmas week, passes which would give them freedom to visit other plantations and be absent from the master's house with permission, were issued to all Negroes. Barring the limitations of these passes, they were free to go anywhere. Some made long journeys, but the majority were content to remain near home. All came back, however, January 2, and settled down on the plantation. Tales of experience and adventure during Christmas week would be indulged in for months afterward, while plans for the "nex" Chris'mas" were already beginning.

When a boy, I was told by an old aunt the story of old Freem and Bob going "sketin' " on glare ice one Christmas Day. There were no skates in the community at that time. Our colored people knew nothing about them. The only "sketin' " they knew about was gliding over the ice on the thick soles of their clumsy shoes. Ice in Missouri in those days, sufficiently thick to skate on, was an unusual thing; but on this particular Christmas Day it was perfect for "sketin'," and many of the Negroes went to the creek to "skete"—young men and young women, old men and old women. It was indeed a gala occasion.

Freem and Bob were well along in years. Freem was subject to rheumatism, and his feet were big and stiff and badly frostbitten. Bob, however, was more nimble, and could "skete" around fairly well. Freem got out into the middle of the glare ice, and he had hard work to keep his feet under him; so he tremblingly stood still. Bob came "sketin' " up to him, and said, "Look a-hyeah, Freem, why don't yu-all skete roun' an' hab lots o' fun, lak ah do?" Freem indignantly replied, "Go, 'long! Ah likes to know how ah's a-gwine to skete roun' when hit am all ah kin do to stay whah ah is."

THE RELATION OF THE WHITE AND BLACK PEOPLE

On our plantation there existed a deep affection in the hearts of the blacks for the whites, and a becoming consideration by the whites for the Negroes. The two composed a large, congenial family, conducting its relations, of course, under the laws of slavery. The colored people of those times were far different from the colored people of today. There is a good reason for its being hard for the younger generation to understand the spirit of those former times.

In the happy, prosperous ante bellum days, the Negroes were proud of their master's family, and loved the individual members of it with a deep devotion. As an illustration of this characteristic of our colored people, I cite the instance of my father's second marriage. My mother died when I was a small boy, and left six children to be cared for by our black mammy. As far as physical care and government was concerned, we had no lack, for she was almost perfect in these essential.

Many and varied are my recollections of this overseer. "Honey," a favored word of the old-time Negro, was used with the most flexible meaning, all depending upon the emphasis and the inflection with which it was spoken. Often it meant something besides "honey." This I knew from many unpleasant experiences. My old black mammy many times laid me across her ponderous knee and spanked me with the most disapproving energy; and after the first half dozen lightning blows, she would ask me in belligerent tones, "Dah now, honey, gwine to do dat any mo'?" If I did not surrender, the act was repeated until I did; but I was always called "honey." She did not mean that I had any characteristics of honey about me, but that I was a little white imp.

But finally my father decided to marry again. None of us children knew of our prospective stepmother until we heard the Negroes talking about her, and they only knew of it through their sagacious observations and their natural ability to discover facts. When father made the announcement to Charles, his valet, and to Ann, his housekeeper, their expressions of delight were ample to make any doubtful suitor feel proud of his achievement in the selection of a companion. Charles said, as he awkwardly fumbled his old soft hat, "Mara James, ah's glad we a'gwine tu be kinfolks tu Mark Bradley's plantation, fu dat's de fines' plantation in all de wo'l'!"

Ann said, "Mah sakes, Massa James, dat li'l', sweet Susan Jane am de only lady in de whole wo'l good nuf to be mothah to Miss Mary's [his first wife's] chillen. Praiz de good Lawd! He am sho' bringin' us one o' His bes' angels."

Then, before father could express any wish as to preparations, Charles apologetically said, "mars James, ah 'spects we bettah fix up dis hyeah place so Missus Susan'll feel glad tu stay wid us." And Ann put in a plea for many new things for us children. It is needless to say she got them all.

From that time to the wedding day, everything about the plantation was changing its complexion from ordinary to extraordinary. The old-fashioned picket fences and all the buildings excepting the residence, were thoroughly whitewashed. Everything was scrubbed and scoured until it fairly sparkled. The carriage horses were groomed several times a day, fed extra, and briskly driven for a while every day by Charles, in order to give them the step and the pep he desired them to have when they went to bring the new mistress to her future home. The harness was redressed, the trimmings polished, the carriage re-painted, and everything set with its best foot forward. Was not an event of the greatest importance about to take place? No detail of preparation was neglected.

When the eventful day dawned, there was joyous intensity in the face of every Negro. Steps were quickened; preparations for the coming of the bride were all completed long before the appointed time, and we children all dressed so father could see how we looked before he left to claim his bride at the Bradley plantation. One would have to see that old-time carriage, with the driver sitting straight and stiff and Charles high up on the footman's seat at the back, in order to get the scene indelibly fixed in mind as I see it today, even after so long a time. Two more important-feeling Negroes never lived. The driver skillfully allowed his whip to touch gently the hips of the spirited steeds as they stood awaiting the word to go, in order to keep them prancing and champing their bits as a matter of effect.

A watch was stationed where he could see the wedding procession coming a half mile away from the home plantation. He gave the signal, and everybody stood at attention. I can never forget the childish imaginations associated with the intensity of that hour. My step mother seemed to be some beautiful fairy, and my father a great king. It was sufficient to inspire in me an everlasting awe and a profound respect for my parents. As the carriage drove up to the plantation gate, our servants voluntarily sprang a surprise on the bridal party. The footman opened the carriage door, and two young colored women stepped forward, forming a saddle of their hands in the old-fashioned way. The footman lifted the bride into it, and she was carried into the house, being immediately followed by my father, borne in the same manner by two young black men.

They were carried to the parlor, and after their wraps were carefully removed by the ones who carried them in, the colored people were permitted to greet the bride. Then they immediately withdrew, and with great pride and enthusiasm made ready to serve the wedding dinner. It was served in plantation style in the spacious dining room, with many guests present. In the evening, the dining room was converted into a ballroom, and the guests danced until a late hour to the music of fiddles and banjos played by several Negroes. In the cabins the colored people, with their guests from the Bradley plantation, were dined and feasted on the leftover delicacies of the wedding dinner, and other food prepared especially for them. I assure you that there was ample for all. Our Negroes knew what to cook and how to cook it. One who has never feasted upon the good things prepared by expert Negro cooks has no conception of real epicurean delights.

While the black people were servants of the whites, their pronounced opinions, together with their known devotion to, and their genuine interest in, the members of the white families, were given due consideration in some of the most important family decisions. Many of the old-time Negroes were the embodiment of natural wisdom.

When a young man came to the plantation to call upon a beloved daughter of the family, he had to come clean if he found favor with these servants, for they were always his first critical examiners. They were ever the first guards to be passed. They usually knew him by reputation, having gained their knowledge from Negroes of other plantations who knew him well. They knew all his good and bad traits of character, and his welcome at their plantation depended upon what they knew from reports, seconded by their own observations. If they did not like him, they of course did not volunteer their adverse opinions to the whites; but they gave free expression to their likes and dislikes in speaking to one another, and these opinions sooner or later came to the ears for which they were intended, and had their influence.

My grandfather had an estimable daughter, Permelia, who took me after my father's death and kept me until I was twenty-one years of age. She told me the following story:

"I had two suitors, a rich plantation owner and a plantation overseer. The overseer's name was O'Bryan. His ancestors had come from Ireland. Mr. Chasteen was the plantation owner. Both of these young men were fine young gentlemen. I liked both of them. My parents preferred the plantation owner, and I thought I did too, at first. They came regularly to visit me—one came one week and the other the next week—for several years.

"Much was made of courtship in those days. There were few hasty marriages. They were not regarded as respectable. When a girl had a beau, he usually remained several days, and a servant was appointed as a valet for him. This Negro had no other duties while the beau was present. I always selected your grandfather's valet for my friends, because he was an expert at the business, and was very dignified in all his ways. Father always seemed to be glad to let me have his valet, and he would take another while my company was there.

"When Mr. Chasteen came, I noticed there was a restraint on the part of my father's valet, though very polite, formal service in every detail was always given. I could not find the least fault with

26

a thing he did, but there was a mysterious reserve ever present with him and with all the other servants.

"When Mr. O'Bryan came, the service was much the same, but the reserve was not there. Whenever these two gentlemen were mentioned, I noticed all the Negroes would speak of Mr. Chasteen only so far as occasion required, but would always enlarge upon the slightest reference to Mr. O'Bryan, by telling of some good thing they had seen in him, or some good report that they had heard about him. I could plainly see which man *they* liked and which they disliked. Then I began to search for the reasons, and gradually I got them.

"As Mr. Chasteen was leaving one Monday morning, after a week-end visit, he handed me a skein of tangled silk to untangle without breaking the thread. That, you know, was an old-time test of a woman's skill and patience. If she untangled the entire skein without breaking it, the lordly man who applied the test would propose marriage to her. If she failed, there would be no proposal. At his next visit he called for the skein of silk as soon as he could with propriety. It had all been untangled without a break, and put up in as attractive a way as I could devise. When he examined it, he was delighted, and said, "That settles it." Then he made a very gallant proposal of marriage. In my most dignified, respectful, ladylike manner, I announced to Mr. Chasteen that the test he had given convinced me he would be a very exacting husband, and I had become engaged to Mr. O'Bryan."

I was thankful things turned out as they did, for Mr. O'Bryan became my foster father, and I could not have possibly loved my own father more. He was a most admirable man—an old forty-niner—and as good a Christian as ever lived. He was the first person I ever heard speak of the second coming of the Lord.

I Remember

THE SLAVE PREACHER AND
THE CIVIL WAR

ONE of the far-reaching influences in plantation life was that of the Negro preacher. He attained his title and standing by the common consent of the colored people themselves. He was not educated in the common meaning of the term, and yet in many ways he seemed to possess quite a practical knowledge in spiritual things. He was not polished in his delivery, but always oratorical and very concrete in the lessons drawn. Nothing could undermine the faith of these men. They were as loyal to God as they were to their masters. Even their infidel masters, if they chanced to have such, could not shake their faith in God nor lessen their devotion to Him.

When a small boy I heard my father tell this story of one Negro preacher and his infidel master:

The preacher was a very highly prized servant, but he persisted in the practice of making audible and long prayers in the barn loft early every morning. This greatly annoyed his infidel master, who usually arrived at the barn on his morning tour of inspection about the time the preacher was at prayer, and he could often hear him praying for "massa."

So one morning the master waited until the preacher had finished his prayer, and then thus addressed him: "Tom, why is it that you so seriously serve a God who does nothing for you? I don't pray, I do not even believe in God, yet I am happy all the time. And I am rich, while you are but a servant. If your God is all you say He is, why doesn't He make you as happy as I am and as rich as I am? Why are you so sad all the time? Why do you have so much trouble?"

The preacher respectfully waited until the master was through and then said, with uncovered head: "Yez, yez, massa, I 'spects hit looks jes' lak dat tu yu; but *dis* am de way it railly am: When you goes duck shootin' an' you shoots a duck and hit drap daid, and you shoots anuddah duck an' jes' wounds hit lak, why does you run aftah de wounded duck and pays no 'tention to de daid duck?"

"Why," said the great duck hunter, "I run after the wounded duck because it might get away. The dead duck will be where it falls when I am ready to go after it."

"Dat am 'zactly de way hit am wid yu an' me, massa. De debble hab got you sho', so he pays no 'tention tu you; but he am not so sho' o' dis hyeah brack chile, so he jes' chases him all de time."

About four years after my father's second marriage, the country was plunged into the Civil War, which brought great suffering and distress to the Southern States. Missouri was a divided State, part free and part slave. South of Mason and Dixon's line slavery was permitted, while north of this line it was not. Our plantation was, of course, south of this dividing line. This situation, complicated and rendered more severe the difficulties usually associated with civil wars. We were on the "firing line" all the time. One day a few hundred Union soldiers would pass, and the next day a detachment of the Southern Army would go by.

These soldiers of both armies did not merely pass, but called on us without fail, and took whatever they wanted, never asking or even thanking us for it. Sometimes it would be a few fat chickens, a fat steer for beef, some hogs, or a few sheep for fresh mutton; and again it would be apples, potatoes, corn, or hay for their horses. One army was as bad as the other. We could discover no difference. They were all lawless, and had no regard for personal rights or property. The Southern Army felt that what we had was theirs, to be used for the defense of the Confederacy. The Union Army regarded us as rebels and acted as if they thought the more they could take or destroy, the sooner the war would be over. The Southern Army would sometimes demand a Negro for a cook, a wagon driver, or for general work; and the Union Army would try to influence the colored people to join the Union Army and, fight for their own freedom. Negroes taken away through these means from our community would, as a general thing, soon come back home. They would slip away form the armies in all manner of ways.. They seemed to prefer to be at home on the old plantations.

The worst things in connection with the Civil War was the many marauding bands of bushwhackers who pretended to be parts of the Southern Army, but who were mere bands of outlaws, robbers, and murderers, going about robbing and killing simply because they could plunder and kill without bring in danger of being punished for their crimes. They hid in the woods and other obscure places during the day, and carried on their depredations during the night.

It was not safe for an able-bodied man to stay at home at night: and he was constantly exposed to danger even in the daytime. If he was a Union man, the regular Southern Army would carry him away as a prisoner of war; or the bushwhackers would come at night and deliberately shoot him. If he was a Southern man, the Union Army would get him on various pretenses. Old men and boys over ten years of age had to "sleep out" nights for fear of being tortured by bushwhackers who sought to secure information about some hidden property or the whereabouts of some neighbor or deserting Negro, wanted for an assumed offense. This torturing was often severe.

Sometimes old men and large boys were shot because they could not, or would not, reveal the information wanted. There lived near our village as fine a white man as ever blessed any community, seventy years of age, foreman in our wool and cotton mill. He did not take sides with either North or South. He did not express himself as for or against either side. He was strictly neutral, and a noncombatant. Two men rode up to his house one afternoon and called him out. They demanded of him, on the penalty of his life, to tell where my father was. He did not know. Father did not tell him or any one else where he was going when he was absent from home in those days. They thought this man did know, but would not tell. So they took him out behind the barn and shot him, and then mounted their horses and deliberately, calmly rode away, leaving the dead man to be buried by the women and boys.

A band of about twenty bushwhackers kicked down our front door one night, and made lights, after they were once inside, by striking matches and throwing the stubs anywhere and everywhere. They took all of my father's private papers, all of his account books, and carried them away. After the war was over, one of our neighbors presented to my father's estate, for settlement, some of these stolen papers. This man was poor when the war broke out, but rich when it ended.

This band of twenty bushwhackers had a young prisoner with them that night—a young boy of about fifteen, whom they had brought to Leesville to point out the location of some valuables. They thought the boy knew where they were hidden. But if he knew, he never told them, for the valuables were not disturbed. After the band left, twenty or more shots were heard about half a mile out of the village in an open strip of prairie. We thought they were simply giving a farewell salute, or firing to intimidate us further, but the next day about 2 P.M. an old Negro noticed several buzzards circling over a definite spot of that prairie. Several of us small boys organized a searching party, and found the mutilated body of the lad the bushwhackers had with them in the village the night before. He had been shot six times in the back. It may be he tried to escape, but it is generally believed that they told him to go, and when he was within good shooting distance, it being dark enough to screen their crime partially, opened fire on him. They did not want him to live as a possible witness against them, for he probably recognized some in the party.

Bushwhackers would stealthily follow a small body of soldiers, and when they found one or two of them separating from the main body, would ambush them. This happened one afternoon near our house. A company of Union soldiers were passing. One young man stopped to see if he could get a little milk.

He seemed to enjoy our company, and stayed until his fellow soldiers were several miles away. As he left, riding by a hedge fence, he was shot by a small band of bushwhackers who had been waiting for such a chance. They shot him in the back of the head as he rode by the hedge behind which they were hiding. They took his horse, his arms, and his clothing, and rode away as fast as they could, fearing their firing might cause some of the soldiers of the main body to come back. Their shots were evidently not heard, for no soldiers returned. An old Negro woman and a boy, who was myself, buried this unfortunate soldier under a young apple tree in the corner of an orchard. He had no coffin. The grave was only deep enough to cover the body about a foot and a half.

Several years after the close of the war, the parents of this young man found out where he was killed and buried. They came to take the body up and remove it to their home somewhere in Illinois. The body was entirely decomposed, having been buried so shallow. The main root of the young apple tree had entered the hole made in the skull by the minnie ball that had killed him, and had followed, with little off-shooting roots, the hollow of the bones down the spine, and run clear to the toes. This linked nearly all the bones solidly together, and the skeleton could be hung up with most of the bones remaining in place.

MY FATHER GIVES HIS SLAVES THEIR FREEDOM AND JOINS THE UNION ARMY

MY FATHER having been born in slavery days, the question of its being right or wrong did not claim his attention until a short time preceding the war. He had always lived on the frontier of the country, and his thoughts were wholly given over to frontier problems. Since there were no newspapers or other means of general communication, matters could not be generally agitated as they are now from one end of the country to the other. He was not, therefore, informed upon the principles of human rights.

But as the war approached, and as he talked with many people passing through our village (our plantation being a stage-coach station), and thought seriously over the matter, he came to recognize the wrong in slavery, though he could not discuss the subject much at home, for all his people and all my stepmother's people were strong Secessionists. His brothers were in the Southern Army, and five of my stepmother's brothers joined the Confederate Army when war was declared. But soon after hostilities began, my father decided he could not fight in defense of slavery, for he saw that its whole system was wrong. So he decided to fight for what he believed to be right, though it meant a very great sacrifice.

I shall never be able to forget, though I continue to try to the end of life, the heart-rending scene of the morning when at breakfast, as the depredations of the marauding bands during the night were being reported by the Negroes through Ann, the all-round housemaid and cook who was serving the meal, my father turned to his beautiful young wife, who had to care for two small children of her own and six of his, the oldest of whom was only fifteen, and said, "I believe old Abe is right, and I feel that my duty calls me to help him to settle the whole business."

True to her inborn Southern womanliness she agreed with her husband's belief in Abraham Lincoln's principles. But there was that large family of small children and the Negroes of the plantation to be looked after and provided for. Besides, all her people believed strongly in the Confederacy, and were bound up with it to the last dollar and the lives of the very flower of their families. The thought of her husband's fighting *against* her five brothers, many dear cousins, and other relatives, as well as against his own near relatives, and the possibility of his never returning, was severe enough to prostrate her delicate body. She soon fell in a faint, and recovered after a long time, but only sufficiently to express her feelings in the most heart-rending groans and moaning that my ears have ever heard. This condition continued for days, long after my father had left to volunteer his services to the Union Army.

Before my stepmother fully recovered consciousness, my father had all the Negroes called together. They stood beneath a

large tree in the plantation yard—a picture I never can forget—
while father announced his plan to join the Union Army and to
set them free. He simply told them he had no more civil or moral right to own them than they had to own him, and that from
that moment they should consider themselves entirely free from
his or any other man's bondage. He told them they could stay
on the plantation if they wished, or they could go somewhere
else. And that he would issue them written releases if they cared
for them. But not one wanted to be released.

As my father made these announcements, the moanings of
my stepmother could be plainly heard through the open windows, and the tears freely coursed down my father's cheeks,
with no effort on his part to wipe them away. They freely bap-
tized that sacred spot consecrated to the cause of freedom. But
his tears were as dew compared with the rain when contrasted
with the tears of the Negroes. They not only shed tears, but
wept aloud, and gave full vent to their feelings. Of course, under
such conditions, all the children, white and black, added their
piercing cries to those of the adults. It was the saddest hour in
all our lives. It was the beginning of the ending of a happy family, never again to be united in this life. It is simply impossible to
express in words the awfulness of such an hour.

When father finished his message to his former slaves, he
told Charles, the negro given to him by his father when he left
home at the age of twenty-one, to saddle "Old Roan," his regular riding horse. He was leaving at once to meet the Union Army, expecting to reach Calhoun, fifteen miles away, that day.
When Charles brought "Old Roan," he also brought another

horse for himself. Nothing father could say or do would shake Charles's purpose to go with him. For the first time in his life this Negro had a mind of his own, with the right to do as he wished. He went with father, and enlisted in the same company as cook, but he insisted upon being father's valet as long as they were together.

Father, having traveled all over that country many times, and being familiar with every road, trail, and almost every hog path of that section of the State, was detailed as a dispatch carrier and scout at the time of Price's raid in northern Missouri—one of the most distressing periods of the Civil War for that State. After being assigned to dispatch work, father rode about fifteen miles to find John Gordon, a young man from the North who had been one of his foremen on the plantation. John was glad to join father as a scout, though he had not yet enlisted. Their experiences the following year would make a large volume of thrilling stories, but omitting all of this, I will at once come to the finishing of father's year of service as a dispatch carrier and general scouting worker.

Father was not a rugged man. He was not accustomed to exposure and irregular meals and impure water. Therefore, when it was necessary for him to ride continuously in a cold rain for three days and three nights, not being off a horse except long enough to change mounts, he was not physically fit for the task. His work was thoroughly done, but near the close of the third day of this long ride, as they were returning to their company headquarters and passing near our plantation, father told Gordon to go on and report to their commander, but stated that he was not able to go any farther.

It was on a cold, raw, rainy, early-twilight fall evening when one of my sisters, sitting by a front window, saw a riderless horse standing at the gate, and looking again, saw a soldier in blue uniform crawling up the walk on his hands and knees. She, of course, was frightened, and ran to our mother and told her what she had seen. We all thought the soldier was creeping upon the house for evil purpose, so the doors were instantly barred and everybody was brought inside for safety. Presently a knock came on the door, and a voice unknown to any of us called for admittance, and declared its identity. But none believed. We thought that it was a trick of an enemy to get into the house. Finally one of the Negroes ventured out of a back door, well armed, and crept around to the front, and to his great surprise found father in a faint on the steps. He had been seized with a severe attack of rheumatism, which finally reached his heart, and he lived only three days after reaching home. He said he wanted to see his family, for he was sure, from what he had already suffered, that he could hardly hope to get through the war alive.

There was only one doctor in the community, a stanch Secessionist, and he attended my father. Three days after my father died, two men rode up through the yard to the front of the house, and called for Mr. Reavis. The small son of the doctor happened to be at the front door when the men rode up, and he told them, in his childish way, that Mr. Reavis was dead, and that he had just been buried. They gave vent to their pleased feelings over this good news by laughing boisterously. They had learned in some way of his arrival home, and had come to kill him. Such was the spirit of the bushwhacker element of those days.

Soon after my father enlisted, and late in the fall, after the crops of the plantation were all gathered in and stored for winter use, a Confederate regiment entered our village during the night and pitched camp in our large plantation yard. They at once began to help themselves to anything they wanted. And their wants included *all we had.* They drove their wagons over the beautiful shrubbery, tore down the artistic yard fence for campfire purposes, went into the henhouse and killed every chicken, turkey, guinea hen, duck, and goose they could find—about five hundred in all—and had a chicken breakfast.

When it was light, they killed a number of fat cattle, sheep, and hogs; and went to the apple and vegetable houses and took all they wanted or could waste. They took all the raw wool and cotton stores in the carding mill, also all spun wool and cotton, all manufactured cloth, and raw and tanned hides. The officers came into our house and took possession, ordered their breakfast prepared by the colored people, they furnishing the turkey, which was taken from our poultry house.

BEHAVIOR OF BOYS AND ANIMALS

THAT same day, twenty-five or thirty soldiers rode out in our pasture with all their rattling paraphernalia to drive in a herd of horses we were keeping there. This herd of horses became very much frightened, and the soldiers had great difficulty in rounding them up in the barnyard. One of the horses was a pet of my eldest sister, who was then in her early teens. He was a very high-spirited horse, and was at the moment greatly excited. He was picked out as the mount for the captain of the company, a fine-looking young Southerner. The horse, all saddled, was brought to the front door of the house for the captain's inspection

The animal was trembling with fright, and my sister threw her arms around his neck and begged for him to be released. But her crying was met with jeers of contempt, and in order to add to her grief, the captain mounted the horse while two men held him. But the minute they let go, the horse began to plunge in the manner of wild Western horses, and finally dislodged the captain, who fell in such a way as to discharge one of the revolvers he had in his belt, and the contents entered his heart. He never spoke again. The horse ran away, and his body was afterward found at the foot of a high bluff in the creek two miles away. He was so frightened he became actually insane. My sister said,

41

"Balllie would rather commit suicide than be a part of the rebel army."

We had another good, gentle horse that my brother and I claimed. He was hardly fit for war purposes, having been badly stifled when young; but to us boys he was the best and most desirable horse on the plantation. The soldiers were going to take him away also. We put up a fight for him. We both got on his back, and refused to get off. They finally pulled us off. We at once climbed back again—a thing we could do with cowboy skill. We were again taken off, with increased roughness, and spanked.

We kicked the soldiers' shins with our hard, calloused bare feet as we cried and pleaded. Our kicking could not hurt the soldiers, but it gave us great satisfaction. They finally quieted us, and then tied the horse to a wagon wheel, and went away to do something else, thinking the matter settled. But as soon as their backs were turned, we loosened the horse and sprang to his back, and gave him our familiar heel touches. He understood when speed was desired, and we were off as fast as the old horse could go.

Some of the soldiers cried out, "shoot the little devils." But they didn't. A soldier mounted a horse and chased us for more than a mile, finally catching us. But we kicked, scratched, and bit until my brother got a chance to snatch the soldier's revolver from his belt and quickly stepped back a few feet and pretended he was going to shoot. The soldier at once surrendered, and promised not only to let us have the horse, but to see to it that we were troubled no more about our pet. He made us promise, however, not to tell anyone how we got the drop on him and forced him to terms. He did not relish the idea of being taken by two small boys, and he did not want his companions to know about it. We readily agreed. All we wanted was our horse, and we got him.

We had a span of mules. They were very large, regular Missouri mules. When young, they had an experience they never forgot. One day we were going to the field to plant corn. The rider of one mule carried a bag of seed corn. The rider of the other carried a tin pail full of water and a tin dipper. They were going lazily along in the hot sun, when all at once the bag became untied and the corn came pouring out, which frightened the mules as they were walking side by side, and they jumped and plunged as only mules can. The riders, being also taken by surprise, were not prepared for such side jumping; so off they went, water, pail, dipper and all. The rattling of the tin pail and dipper, with water splashing all over the mules, added to their fright. After that we could never carry anything that had a tin rattle to it on either of them. They did not care for the rattle of anything else, but they drew the line on tin.

Two soldiers came to me one day as I was plowing with this fine team of mules, and ordered me to take them out. I tried to explain to them that they were worthless to them because they had been spoiled, but they would pay no attention to what I said. I unharnessed, and the soldiers unsaddled their old, worn-out horses, and flung their saddles, bedecked with tin cups and tin canteens, onto the mules. They humped up their backs, and swelled out in regular mule fashion, but stood perfectly still until the men mounted them. Then they began to plunge as they had done on the day when the bag of seed corn surprised them, and the soldiers fortunately fell in the soft dirt where I had been plowing. Then they commanded me to catch the mules, so they could get their saddles off. I had a hard job, because every time the mules would move, the tin contraptions would rattle, and away they would go again. But after a long time I succeeded in catching one of them. The other, running furiously through the apple orchard, unsaddled herself, and was calm after the rattle was gone. The soldiers resaddled their old horses and rode away, muttering contemptuous things to themselves, and leaving me the most delighted boy in all the Southern States. This team of mules was taken from us a number of times, but always came back as undesirable. What a fortunate day for us when the bag of seed corn was spilled!

This particular group of soldiers stayed with us for several days. And they were hectic days! Then they heard the Union Army was coming; so they finished cleaning us out by our horses and mules, cows and cattle, all fruit and vegetables, and corn,—everything we had, —and left a young wife with eight small children and about a dozen colored people at the beginning of winter, with but little to wear and without a thing to eat excepting *one sack of corn hominy and five boxes of hardtack* one of the Negroes had succeeded in hiding.

There was no Red Cross nor any other relief organization to come to our rescue. We had to shift for ourselves, and it was a struggle against cold and hunger not equaled by any modern calamities over which much is made, millions of dollars spent, and thousands of hearts wrung in sympathetic agony. And yet, as I review those days of deprivation, I cannot recall any of our sufferings that appear to be so great in this conception of the present public mind as the privations of people nowadays who, according to all local circumstances, could not be in nearly so great need. Today people are reported as starving when they are only shorn of luxuries, and as ruined for life if they do not have bread and milk. They would die of contracted diseases if exposed to cold day and night throughout an entire winter. But I and seven other young children went through several severe winters without shoes and with very scant clothing of any kind.

And we had to be out in the weather much of the time in search of fuel and food. Bread was not even seen at one time for the space of three months, much less tasted. We had no salt, no fats of any kind, except a limited quantity of black walnuts which we gathered form the woods. We happened at this particular time, however, to have sweet potatoes, on which we lived, without butter or any other seasoning, for three months, and came through in good health. But I have never liked sweet potatoes since! Nobody died while going through all this deprivation, and none died soon after. All lived to a reasonable old age. Some are past seventy years of age, and are still in good health, and generally more active than many at that age who never had a winter's chilling with only a scant allowance of walnuts and sweet potatoes as food.

It is wonderful what an unpampered child can go through without permanent injury. We did not die, but on account of the almost constant presence of some kind of soldiers in the house and in all the other plantation buildings, we had vermin of all kinds to the extent that we were almost devoured by them. We also had the seven-year itch, and to my best recollection, it ran true to its name—seven years.

This general deplorable condition continued for about two years, and ended in so far as pertained to lack of food and clothing, when three of our relatives on my father's side came and took his first wife's children home with them into a part of Missouri not then so severely afflicted by extreme war conditions, and yet even more harassed by bushwhackers. This was the finishing act of breaking up the family begun by the sorrowful day my father set his slaves free and rode away to join the Union Army.

No man or woman who has never gone through the actual experience of being taken in childhood from his own home, no matter how humble that home may have been, can have any conception of the feelings of the child thus taken—not so much at the immediate time of separation, but afterward. The days, weeks, months, and even years of silently borne loneliness are far worse on health and mind than are lack of food and clothing. Yet when a child has gone through such an experience, the ordinary trials of his future life have but little discouraging effect upon him. Such experiences prepare him for patiently and ever joyously bearing the common, everyday trials. By all these experiences I have been taught how it can be that the "all things" can work together for good. There is no trial or grief so great or severe that our heavenly Father cannot make it a blessing to the stricken one. Orphans, as a general thing, did not have the handicaps of the present-day "coddling," which is a greater calamity for them than all the ravages of war.

During the war, the boys of all communities in the South

played soldier a great deal. It was not altogether play, either, for frequently there was severe, actual fighting. Boys were divided according to the politics of their parents. There were always more Secessionists in our part of the State than Union boys. Both sides were well organized, according to boy-army regulations. Whenever the two sides met, there was sure to be a real fight. Our implements of warfare were guns, pistols, and swords made of wood. I first learned to use tools such as we had in making arms for our "army." There was no actual shooting, because, of course, wooden guns were only imitations, but there was a lot of bayoneting, and sword slashing, and hard punching with wooden implements. Oftentimes when a battle was over, the boys were a ruffled, dirty, bleeding lot. I still possess several large scars on my body which serve as reminders of those early boy struggles for freedom, and many of the others in the group can boast of even more scars than I.

Our public school teacher was a strong Secessionist. He was quite lame, else he would have been forced into the Southern Army. One day at noon the captain of the juvenile Union Army got into a rough scuffle (a thing not unusual) with the captain of the rebel army on the school playground. The captains were evenly matched in strength and fighting qualities. The teacher, in separating them, struck the Union captain a severe blow in the face, whereupon the whole Union gang, who were watching the struggle of the contestants, sprang on the teacher and left him unable to conduct the school that afternoon, and many of the boys were in as bad shape as he was. It was a great Union victory. Before school-time next morning the teacher left the village without notice. The school was broken up, and was not reorganized until after the close of the war three years later.

The boys of that place who were too large to be harmless and too young to enlist, were to be reckoned with in all community affairs. To illustrate how the boys ruled in many things, I cite the case of the son of a man who was a bushwhacker, a robber on a large scale. This boy was about fourteen years of age. He afterward became an evangelist known all over the United States and in many foreign countries. The father would make frequent trips from home, and usually return with several four-mule teams, hauling wagons loaded with all manner of valuable goods. On one occasion he came loaded with wool yarn, which was very scarce and almost priceless. It was far more desired than money itself, for it took a great deal of money to buy a very small amount of yarn, and besides, there was no yarn in that immediate part of the country.

In our community were several very poor women with a lot of children about them—women whose husbands were in the army, and two whose husbands had been killed. They were quite destitute.

This robber was very weary upon his return from this trip. He had evidently made a long, hard journey. So he and his gang slept all of the first day after their return. This gave his son a good opportunity to inspect the wagons and their plunder. Finding the wool yarn and knowing its value and the need of it in the village, he took a generous supply to every poor family as a present. They could hardly account for this generosity nor understand it; so they questioned the boy closely. He was very frank, telling them plainly that his father had stolen it and was going to market it at a high price, but that it was not his father's legitimate property, and therefore they could have all they wanted—all they would take.

They refused to accept it, but he left it with them in spite of their protest. They reported the boy to his father the next day, and the father asked his son for an explanation. The boy's reply was: "Father, you took the yarn for gain for yourself. I gave it away for the gain of the needy. It was not your rightful property. I have not robbed you, but you have robbed others." The yarn was left where the boy had put it, and the father made no more foraging trips.

In a way the large boys during the Civil War were the unorganized and unrecognized home guards, and at the same time the chief providers of the little their families had in the way of food and clothing.

I Remember

MY INTRODUCTION TO
HEALTH REFORM

BUT, as I have said, my father's relatives came and took the older of us children away from the old plantation. Two sisters and I went home with Aunt Permelia O'Bryan,—the same aunt who had once untangled the skein of silk,—and a better woman never lived. She was a devoted Christian—a strict Sunday observer. Instead of letting me go off swimming Saturday afternoons with the neighborhood boys, she would make me chop wood for Sunday's use—a thing I never relished doing, knowing the other boys were down in the old swimming hole having a wonderful time. But that made no difference. The wood was cut !

Aunt was also a strict old-time health reformer, an ardent disciple of one Dr. Trall. "Cold water and two plain meals a day" was her hobby, and she rode it hard. Also every one else in her home was compelled to ride the same steed. On her farm, nobody got more than two meals a day. That we were up at 4 A. M. and breakfast at six and dinner at twelve the year round made no difference. After dinner was served, under no circumstances did we get more food of any description until the next morning.

I used to be so hungry at night I would dream of eating and never getting enough. Aunt would frequently quote the saying,

"Breakfast is gold; dinner is silver; and super is lead." I used to think some of the lead would be delicious to me, and wonder at what hour of the night the supper lead became breakfast gold. To me, supper became the most desirable thing I could imagine. Yet to indulge would have seemed to me to be almost criminal. However, I still remember one transgression, and my subsequent confession, that I had secretly eaten some "hoecake"— plain, cold-water corn bread—one night after running cattle all day without dinner.

I was never reconciled to the two-meal plan; and yet under it I developed from a puny dwarf to a hearty, strong, robust youth. It must have been for me more beneficial than pleasant. I had always been a puny, sickly boy—a regular runt. This recalls an interesting incident.

As a child I was not taught to pray. We had no family worship, and I never heard my parents, nor any one else, pray. But in some unaccountable way I knew about prayer, perhaps through the Negro servants. When the almost unendurable attacks of stomachache to which I was subject came, I generally went upstairs in the loom house and lay on the pile of ever-present carpet rags and prayed for relief. Then I would usually fall asleep, because, the pain being so intense, I became exhausted. Sometimes the family would be searching for me when I awoke, and of course I would be required to account for my absence. This was a delicate situation for me, for I was sure I would not be believed if I told the truth.

One day, however, the housemaid saw me go into the loom house, and she took the trouble to spy. She slipped in quietly and heard me softly crying and praying upstairs, and went and brought my mother to hear for herself. That day I slept unusually long. In fact, I was carried into the house before I awoke. That was the end of stomach trouble with me. I have never had occasion to know, through pain of any kind, that I have a stomach since that time. I have always believed that the Lord heard and answered my childish prayer, and thoroughly healed me not only of that trouble, but of others also.

Just a few years before I went to live with her, Aunt Permelia had recovered from a long spell of sickness. For months she had been confined to her bed, and the doctors could do nothing for her. But she regained her health through this Dr. Trall's system of dieting and cold-water treatments. It was natural, therefore, for her to be zealously favorable to his methods, not only in recovering health, but in maintaining it.

To illustrate how zealous she was, I give this instance: G. H. Rogers, father of H. E. Rogers, General Conference statistician, was staying at our house while moving his gospel tent into our neighborhood, preparatory to holding a series of meetings. He had an early breakfast, and worked hard all day, and returned at ten o'clock at night. He asked Aunt Permelia for something to eat, saying he was so hungry he was faint. She promptly replied: "That will never do. You just take a drink of cold water and go to bed, and you will be all right in the morning." He laughingly obeyed.

There was another forced practice under which I seemed to develop physically. This other dreaded practice was a cold bath every morning, summer and winter. These cold baths were not objectionable during the warm weather. But with such poor accommodations as we had on the farm, the limit came in the wintertime. Always my last chore of the day was to draw a big tub of water for the family's ablutions the next morning; The well was some distance from the bath shed, built back of the house, so the water had to be carried from the well to the bath shed the night before to save time in the morning and added exposure in cold weather.

The bath shed was not wind proof, neither was it heated in any way. It was as cold as a barn. Into that cold shed I had to march as soon as I got up out of a warm bed every morning, and take a cold splash. Sometimes the tub of water ran the night before would be frozen over the top. In such an emergency I used a stick of stove wood to break the ice. But the bathing had to go on as usual, no matter about the temperature of the water or the frigidity of the weather. Aunt seemed to think the baths should always be as cold as the weather. It would seem to some that such treatment would kill a person, but it did not kill any of us. Indeed, we scarcely ever had even a cold. Doctors never had a call to the O'Bryan home all the years I was there.

THE BUSHWHACKER PERIL AND
ARMY RAIDS

URING the last two years of the Civil War, bushwhacking had increased to such an extent that the country was full of these lawless, pilfering bands. They lived by plundering. They were highwaymen taking anything and everything they wanted, and killing men upon the most trivial excuses. I never heard of their killing any Southern men who were in full sympathy with the secession, however. To avoid these bands, the elderly white men, the Negro men who were at home for various reasons, the large boys, and all young men who had not enlisted, would "hide out" nights, winter and summer. Their hiding places had to be changed frequently to prevent neighborhood knowledge of the place of concealment. Nobody could be trusted in those times, not even apparently friendly neighbors.

One dark, rainy night a band of bushwhackers came to my aunt's home, which was on a main thoroughfare in a prairie country, surrounded by a large field of corn then in tassel. They were after my cousin, a young man twenty-two years of age, who had been attending college in Illinois. They had heard of his return, and knowing he was in sympathy with the North, they planned to surprise him on this night, and to make away with him. All the Negroes, old and young men, and boys hid that night in a forty-acre field of corn—away out in the middle of the corn. The corn was quite thick, and in keeping with wartime cultivation, the weeds were even thicker than the corn, and nearly as high. It was really a good hiding place.

The hiders always kept close together, and one of them watched while the others slept. The bushwhackers had evidently been informed of our location that night, for they began at one side of the field and rode their horses in every other row clear across and through the entire field. The watch awakened us when he heard the tramping of the horses passing at a distance back and forth and up and down the rows of corn, which were a quarter of a mile long. Our blankets were snugly rolled up for emergency moves. It was noticed that each time the riders passed the center of the field, they were two or three hundred feet closer to us, so it was decided that they were combing the field thoroughly. Finally they passed us at an uncomfortably short distance, and while they were near the end of the field an eighth of a mile away, we made a dash far into that part of the field they had covered in their search, and again listened to them pass and repass, as they got farther and farther away, until they finally reached the other side. Then they made a charge upon a plum thicket about a quarter of a mile distant. We had been hiding there for several weeks before the return of my cousin. But we were not there that night; so they gave up the search and rode away.

The next day a neighbor, who lived about three miles distant, came over to see, so she said, whether we were all right, for the same band of bushwhackers were at her home before they called on us, and told her there would be at least one less Yankee before sunrise next morning. She was very solicitous about how and where we gave them the slip, but she did not find out anything that would help the bushwhackers in their next attempt on the life of my cousin. She had only been gone a short time when we saw, coming over the ridge in the prairie, a long column of cavalry. It proved to be a part of a Union Army stationed thirty miles away. When they learned of the visit of the bushwhackers and of the visit of the woman who called on us, the captain sent one of my sisters over to this woman's house. She was to tell her in a very diplomatic way that our men would hide that night in the apple house in the orchard. The woman thought that would be a fine place, for the bushwhackers would not thing of going there, because it was not apple season, and naturally was too near the house.

The Union soldiers marched away in broad daylight, but twenty of them came back after dark, hid their horses in the cornfield, and took lodging in the apple house. About 1 A. M. the bushwhackers crept up close to the apple house, and nearly all of them fell at the first volley of the Union soldiers, who had cut portholes in the walls through which to fire. The leader of the gang, who was severely wounded, proved to be the husband of the woman who pretended to be so much interested in our safety.

The winter following this experience, as we all sat before a log fire in the early evening, the windows darkened with heavy bed quilts and all doors securely barred, there was a sudden crash at the front door. It was crushed with a fence rail, and five bushwhackers came rushing in. All of our men quickly dodged into a dark back room, ran up a ladder into a low loft, pulling the ladder up after them, and gently let the blind trap door slide into place again. I did not succeed in making my escape, for I was too frightened to think of anything; so they got me.

This time they came for a new saddle they seemed to know we had. Of course, we evaded any direct or satisfactory answer, but they said they positively knew we had one, and they were going to have it, or burn us out. We thought of our men in the attic in case our home was fired, but my old aunt, two sisters, and I still did not reveal anything of a new saddle about the place. We showed them all the old saddles, and told them they were welcome to any or all of them, but they swore at us and demanded the *new* saddle. They looked everywhere about the house in vain, and then ordered me to get a lantern and go with two of them out to the old log stables some distance from the house. This was a terrible ordeal for me, for I was afraid they would kill me out there. And I really did *not* know where the saddle was. They thought I knew all about it, but would not tell them in the presence of my aunt.

When we went into the stable, one big, surly fellow drew a big army revolver out of his belt, and in the cocking process it made two sickening, deathly clicks I shall never forget. He pointed it right into my face, and with guttural oaths demanded that I tell him at once where the saddle was. I wished I did know its location, for the real value of the saddle, though very great at that time, seemed to be a very small thing to me just then. I knew also some boys of my age had been killed by bushwhackers. But I was small for my age, and did not know at that time that threats of violence were often made for the sole purpose of extracting information wanted. I thought these men intended to do all they said they would to me if I did not tell them where the saddle was hidden. It was very real to me. All I could do was to cry and insist that I *did not know*!

By that time the other man had taken a rope plow line from the harness hooks and said to the man with the gun, "Wait a minute. Don't shoot him yet. We will *choke it* out of the little lying imp. We will swing him up on this beam until he will be glad to tell all he knows. He does not seem to be afraid of a gun, but this hemp line will choke the truth out of the little devil."

So they put the rope around my neck, and jerked me around in a very rough way for some time, and then threw the line over the beam and began to pull me up. I do not know what happened then, for when I seemed to awaken, the line was not around my neck, and one of the men said to me in a very soothing, friendly, patronizing tone, "Now we will go back to the house, and tell your smart old aunt that you told us where the saddle is, and for her to get it, or we will kill all of you by burning the house with all of you in it."

I said to him, "I cannot tell my aunt that I told you where the saddle is, for I really truly do not know where it is."

"Then tell her to get it for us quick, for we are going to burn all of you if she doesn't give us the saddle at once!"

When we returned to the house, I told my aunt, as best I could, what they had told me to tell her. She gave me a quick, searching look, and without further hesitation, told them where the saddle was hidden, for she saw that I had passed through some fearful ordeal while in the stable, and knew we were dealing with a murderous gang who would do all they threatened if the saddle was not delivered to them. She at once decided our lives were of more value than even a costly saddle.

When they got the saddle, they brought it into the house and very deliberately and admiringly examined it, and became very

Congenial and apologetic, especially to me. They went away, but the next morning I found an old saddle set up on the top of the large front gatepost. They had left this in exchange for what they had taken. This old saddle was used on the farm up to the time I left at the age of twenty but I never looked at it without a flashing thought of the trying experience I had passed through on the night it came to us.

About this time Gen. Sterling Price, of the Southern Army, made a raid in the State, and the Union Army sent thousands of soldiers out to defeat him. Soldiers were everywhere. One day a large body of Southern soldiers would pass, and the next day a Union Army contingent would pass. A detachment from each army would invariably give us a call and demand food. If the Union Army thought we were Unionists, they would graciously accept whatever we offered them, but would not forcibly take anything. The Southern Army was fully as considerate of those whom they regarded as Secessionists. So we fared better, in that we could keep the little food and the few cattle, horses, sheep, and hogs we had, when we could give the impression that we were favorable to whichever army was at the moment passing on the highway. Merely for protection, my sister and I would get on the big front gateposts whenever we saw an army approaching, and as soon as we could determine who they were by the color of their uniform, we began to wave and to shout as only lusty children can, for either North or South. And we soon learned we could have a fine time with the soldiers as they passed. Usually an orderly would be stationed at the gate by the officer leading the column to keep the soldiers from trespassing upon the premises. When all had passed, the orderly would bid us a pleasant farewell and gallop to the front of the column again.

Price's raid left the country destitute. No corn, wheat, or oats remained. The mills were burned. From June to September that year we had no bread of any kind in our home, neither had we any meat or green vegetables—nothing except early sweet potatoes. We had plenty of these, however; but we ate them alone, boiled or baked, without salt, butter, milk, or sugar, for three long months.

The first piece of bread I saw after this long fast was made from grated corn before it was fully ripe. The meal was simply mixed with water, and baked on the hearth on the lid of an iron vessel with coals of fire under it—a fine way to bake break when the dough is properly prepared. But just coarse, grated meal, with large pieces of grains of corn all through it, mixed with water and no salt, no shortening of any kind, could not be expected to compare with good bread, even though it was baked in an approved manner. And yet, after all these years, I can truthfully say that I have never relished any bread as I did that first grated loaf after a three months' bread fast. To this day I recall its all-round deliciousness, and in my memory it remains the most delectable food I ever ate.

During Price's raid through Missouri there was devastation on every hand. Houses were ruthlessly burned, and property of all kinds was destroyed. All stock was reduced almost to extinction. It was a time of unlimited death and destruction. Only old men, young boys, girls, and women were left. Only undesirable live stock could be kept, and even much of this was needlessly destroyed. The country as a whole was far more stricken than some of the countries injured by the recent World War, yet there were no charitable organizations collecting food, money, and enlisting sympathy for us. We did not expect it, did not even think of such a thing. We solved our own problems, and in time met our own needs and came out the stronger as the result of our trying experiences and difficulties.

THE RELATION OF THE WHITE AND THE COLORED PEOPLE—AFTER THE WAR

THE closing of the Civil War left people of the South poor, very poor, and thousands of Negroes homeless and destitute. Had it not been for the kind consideration of the white people of the South, many of these helpless colored people would have miserably perished. They had been dependent upon white people all their lives, and did not know how to plan for themselves. And to a large degree the white element was not accustomed to doing hard manual labor. They had merely directed it. So the Negroes were still needed by their former owners, and certainly this need was fortunate for them. But their relations had now suddenly been changed, and a new, strange order of things had to be met and adjusted. This was no small undertaking. It involved many perplexities which the Northern people did not and could not appreciate. Former servants had become free men and women. They were no longer the property of their one-time masters.

This new relationship turned the heads of many of the younger element among the Negroes. But the more mature colored people retained their old-time general demeanor, and they fared far better than the others.

In slavery times the colored people were fed well according to the standard of good food at that time. They were clothed comfortably. They had plain, comfortable cabins. They were treated kindly, as a general rule. True, some were punished when they willfully transgressed well-known regulations, but corporal punishment was a common method of correction for any offender against the law, no matter what his color, at least in our neighborhood. And white children were punished quite as often as were the colored children. In my judgment, a little more physical chastisement today and less imprisonment would work far better reformations. Some people like to be fed and housed at the expense of the community they offend.

But while the Southern white people, in our part of the country, were kind to the colored people, certain social distinctions existed. On this point there has ever been, and probably always will be, a difference of opinion between the two races.

To illustrate how Southern White people in the south related themselves to the Negroes within ten years after the war, I will give an instance of my own experience. When I landed at Battle Creek College late in the afternoon on a cold day in January, 1875, I was taken to the home of one of the devout members of the Battle Creek church to room and board. I retired early that night, as I had been traveling the two previous nights, and sleeping cars and dining cars were not used by the common people then as they are today.

The next morning I was a little tardy in getting down to

breakfast. All the boarders were seated at the long dining table, waiting for me, when I opened the stairway door leading into the room. In compliance with custom, the host had all the plates stacked at his end of the table, with the dishes containing food in front of him. And he forthwith, without asking whether any of us wanted what he had to serve or not, began to load every plate with two boiled potatoes, and a large fat boiled onion, over all of which he poured a generous supply of thick, white gravy, and passed this plates thus filled down the two sides of the table.

There was present a pronounced offensive odor, the likes of which I had never smelled before. It was sickening, but I did not know what it was. As my plate sat steaming before me, I discovered that it came from the food itself. But others were eating with evident relish, and I was game. However, it was soon necessary for me to excuse myself, for I was really sick. I hurried back to my room upstairs, being closely followed by the good housewife, who manifested great concern for my well-being. She inquired whether I was accustomed to fainting spells, and suggested sending for one of the sanitarium doctors who lived near by. Poor woman, she did not know that the cause of my present sickness was the combination of boiled onions, which I always detested, and codfish gravy, the odor of which I had never before smelled. These two articles of Northern diet were too much for me, especially for breakfast. I wondered if that was a fair sample of the kind of food Michigan people lived on, and resolved that if it were, I would soon be back in my native State. I was not only sick with an offended stomach, but I was homesick and discouraged.

We had no onions or codfish for dinner, and having existed

for several days upon lunches, I was hungry enough to eat fairly well, even when things I did not relish were passed to me.

At this lodging house was a young colored man who was working for his board while going to school. He was clever enough to discern the cause of my sickness at that first morning breakfast, for he had had the same experience with these two foods, of which this particular family was very fond. He came to my room and assured me that I would become tolerant toward such a diet in time if I did not become mentally antagonistic because of this unfavorable introduction. He first taught me the importance of one's mental attitude upon any question under consideration. In his simple was of stating it, he said: "You all knows we kin think a thing is bad, and it sho is bad; or we kin think a thing is good, and by'n by hit gets good. You all 'members dat do Good Book sez a man is jist what he thinks he is. So I specks even onions and codfish is good if we thinks they is." This young man was wise in practical things, but deficient in what we call book learning. He was poor, and had been unable to go to school until he was about my age, and then only by working hard every spare moment.

Being accustomed to helping colored people whenever and wherever they needed assistance, I helped this boy for one hour each evening with his lessons for the following days, since I was in advanced classes. I gave him money for books and clothes and took a general interest in him. And he had enough real African blood in his veins to appreciate keenly all favors and reciprocate wherever opportunity offered.

One morning, as I came to the door of the college building, I was met by a gang of bright, well-attired city young men, to whom I was apparently a queer specimen of humanity. My clothes were in frontier style, and my Missouri drawl and general appearance were really amusing to these city chaps. They accosted me that morning as had been their custom for some time in the past, and were having really an amusing time among themselves at my expense, when this young colored student appeared around the corner of the building. He listened to these young men for only a short time, and then laying aside the books I had bought for him and removing his gloves, stepped up to the leader of the gang, who afterward became a prominent man in our general work and a good friend of mine, and told him a few polite yet emphatic things in the hearing of all his pals. And from that day until the time Battle Creek college closed the doors as an educational institution, there was no more hazing of that or any other sort. A colored boy had effectively put an end to a thing the faculty had not been able to overcome.

This is an actual experience of a young Southern man with a young colored man ten years after the close of the Civil War, and answers the question relative to the normal relations of the white and colored races after the war. Of course there were extremists in both races, but among the best elements there never was any marked inconsiderateness upon the part of either for the other.

I Remember

STOGY, MY CONTRABAND HORSE

NEAR the close of the war, horses and mules, aside from those used in the army, were very few. Only the very poorest, those wholly unfit for war purposes, could be found anywhere.

One day after a large army had passed our place, from a distance of one quarter of a mile across the prairie, I saw a horse stretched out by the side of the road. I thought he was dead, yet I had heard no gunshot, as we often heard when disabled horses were of necessity left behind. I went out to investigate, and found the poor horse more dead than alive, but he was simply worn out and starved. His back was covered with ugly saddle sores. His hoofs were worn to the quick, and he was little more than skin and bones. He had evidently stepped into a deep hog root, and being weak and exhausted, fell under his rider, and in falling, had sprained his right hind leg so badly he could not get up. So after the saddle and bridle had been removed, he was left to die where he had fallen.

I went back to the house and brought two buckets of water and some rags with which to wash his sores. He was very thirsty, and drank as best he could lying down. I bathed his head and washed his back, leaving the wet rags on the sores while I gathered grass for him to eat. I got him all the things I could find which I knew horses like to eat. I bound up his injured leg, and kept it wet with cold water. The next morning he was stronger, having had a good night's rest, and all he could eat; but he could not get up. A horse, you know, gets up on his forefeet first, and needs two good strong hind legs to lift his hind quarters. He had only one hind leg he could use, and the lame one seemed to be very much in his way.

I decided to have a "raising." I got my sisters, my aunt, Mammy Ann, and our old colored man, and armed with a strong fence rail, we called on the contraband horse. He almost seemed to know what we wanted to do, for he willingly did all he could to help us. We lifted him up on his forefeet, and then put the fence rail under his flanks, and all of us lifted as we appealed to the horse to do his part. And id did, though it evidently caused him much pain. From that moment on, that horse and I were the best of friends. I hugged his neck and patted his head, and was profuse in words of tenderness to him and denunciations for those who had treated him so harshly. He showed his approval of all I said and did, by resting his nose on my shoulder.

It was a slow, hard journey to our humble stables. The horse had to make it on three legs. Once in the stable, I tied him up with ropes, attaching them to the beams of the hayloft. He could not lie down, but could rest his full weight on the many strands of rope extending from the beams down under his body and back up to the beams on the opposite side of him—a rope sling in which he could both stand and recline. He was kept in this sling until he gave evidence that his lame leg was well enough to allow a partial use of it. In a remarkable short time he was quite strong and spirited. He was only four years old, and of a fine breed.

Then I was uneasy about his being taken from me by some marauding band of robbers. So I had to hide him out nights, and keep a sharp lookout in the day time, lest some band slip up on us and take him. But the war closed, and most of the horse thieves infesting the country immediately thereafter were soon hanged or driven out; so my hard-earned, highly prized war contraband thoroughbred was saved. He was of the Morgan stock, and seemed to have more than ordinary "horse sense." But he was ever a war horse, for the smell of powder and the sound of a gun made him nervous.

At that time, rabbits were a great pest to farmers in our part of Missouri. All farms were enclosed by Osage orange hedges, which grew thick and very rapidly. The sharp thorns on the branches made the hedge formidable to all large animals, but a defense to all small creatures, especially rabbits. Neither wolves nor dogs nor any other rabbit-eating animals could reach the rabbits in these hedges. So there they took up their abode, and bred very rapidly. They ate the tender corn as fast as it came up. Garden truck could not be raised at all unless fenced in with rabbit proof picket fence. (There were no such things as wire fences in those days.) Also, the rabbits would bark all young fruit trees and kill them. The great thing to be achieved, therefore, was the extermination of the rabbits. Killing them became part of the business of the farmer. All leisure hours were devoted to this end. Rabbits stay in hiding during the day. They feed during the early part of the night, coming out of their runs about sunset, and earlier just after rains.

71

I Remember

Late in the afternoon of a warm July day a very hard rain-
storm came up, and it rained as only is could rain in those days
when the country was new and very thinly settled. But just before sundown it cleared up, and everything was in its prime.
Even the rabbits came out in droves to welcome the freshness.
My uncle suggested that we boys shoot rabbits for a little pas-
time. Another boy about my age and general make-up was
working on the farm for his board and clothes that year. This
suggestion was pleasing to both of us, since shooting at anything
was our hobby. We had a lot of old army muskets, revolvers,
and, strange as it may seem to our readers, in our great, war-
imposed poverty, we always had an abundance of ammunition.
We were never poor in powder, bullets, caps, and guns. The soldiers during the war always paid boys for any special favors in
old guns and ammunition. We had a regular arsenal in our
home.

On this particular occasion we decided to use revolvers, two
each. They were large six-shooters, old army style. We took the
four revolvers and went out by the stable to load up. As we ex-
citedly jabbered while we loaded, about how many rabbit hides
we would stretch on the smokehouse door on this one auspi-
cious occasion, Stogy, my revived war-time Morgan horse, being
loose in the lot, poked his wise nose down between us as we sat
on the ground, and took a whiff of the powder-fumed revolvers,
then looked straight at me with a queer expression in his eyes,
and I thought he said by his looks, "What does all this mean?
Are you small boys going to war?" "No, Stogy," I said, "no real
war in it for us, only some fun shooting rabbits." Then I tickled
him under the chin where the nit flies find horses so sensitive to

touch, and banteringly and playfully said to him, "Don't you wish you were a little man-boy instead of just a horse-boy, so you could go shoot rabbits too?" He gave a little squeal and plunged around the lot several times, stopping to give a big snort occasionally. The smell of the powder about the guns evidently had some unusual influence upon him. His general actions suggested to us the idea of getting on Stogy, and rushing right out into the prairie grass among the rabbits, and shooting right and left. This was a boy's fancy, rather than practical good sense. But it was a pleasing idea, and Stogy was enlisted. He seemed to be a bit nervous, but in every way willing.

I put a plain bridle on him and we mounted his bare back. His big fat sides made our short legs spread out at an angle of about 45degrees. But while he was full of life, and appeared to be dangerous, he was very gentle, and absolutely dependable. We had no fear of him. We rode out of the stable lot through the large farmyard, out of the front gate, through a short lane, and into a stretch of prairie skirted by a hedge fence for a quarter of a mile. The prairie was literally alive with rabbits, partially hidden from view by a luxurious growth of grass averaging from six to ten inches high. We headed Stogy for a parallel run with the hedge, but well out in the grass. The bridle reins were dropped on his shoulders and the word was given for him to go! He was evidently anticipating something out of the ordinary, and was ready for the word the instant he got it. As soon as he reached the rabbit-infested grass, we began firing, bang, bang, bangity bang, bang , bang! In rapid succession, and Stogy straightened himself parallel with the ground, as he had been accustomed to doing in cavalry charges in his war days. He acted as if he were in real war work, and fairly flew across that prairie, away out into the center of the plain, gaining momentum with every bound.

We were busy shooting as fast as we could pull the triggers of the guns, and Stogy was absorbed in his running, and none saw or even thought of the wet-weather gully that coursed through the center of the prairie and was almost entirely concealed by tall grass. It was running flush with its banks after the hard rain. Stogy did not see it until he was only a few feet from it—too late to stop, even if he had had the stop idea, which he did not have. He must clear it in one tremendous bound, and he did, but we didn't. We landed, guns and all, in one big splash in the fast-running, muddy water, and Stogy sailed on riderless, until he thought the war was over, the firing having ceased as we boys plunged into the water. We climbed out as best we could, but our guns were at the bottom of the branch, and must stay there until the water had all run out a few hours later.

We were a curious-looking pair of dilapidated, water-soaked rabbit killers—enough to make a horse laugh; and we thought Stogy did laugh as he came loping back to us, soon after we had got out of the water and captured our old straw hats some distance down the stream. We demurely remounted Stogy and slowly made our way back to the house, where we were first met in the yard by Mammy Ann, who aroused the whole family with her loud exclamations and derisive comparisons. Stogy was the only one of the three who seemed to enjoy the situation. My aunt came running out of the house, expecting to find some awful calamity. But when she found we were only wet and exceedingly muddy, she chided my uncle for allowing us to go on such a dangerous adventure. She said, with great agitation, that we might have shot ourselves and Stogy too. Uncle calmly assured her there was not the slightest danger of our hitting ourselves, stogy, nor even a rabbit.

"BANG, BANG, BANGITY, BANG, BANG, BANG!"

EXPERIENCES WITH STOGY

TWO years later my uncle purchased 160 acres of prairie land fifty miles east of Kansas City and seven miles north of Holden, which was then a division of the Missouri Pacific Railway. We moved up there in the old-time way—covered wagons, each drawn by four mules and followed by a drove of sheep and cattle, with a belled cow tied to the rear wagon, and my two sisters and I on horseback following to keep the stock bunched in the trail and to prevent loss of any through straying. (All country girls in those days were expert horse-women. They rode on sidesaddles, and wore ling riding skirts. My sisters could chase cattle on the open prairie as well as any man.) There were 150 cattle, composed of cows, yearlings, and two-year-olds, and 200 sheep.

Sheep are easy to drive when they have a good leader. Cattle have to be constantly driven and kept rounded up. They seem to be endowed with a straying disposition, and some of ours constantly persisted in following that inclination. They rebelled against being driven at times, and staged a contest between the power of man to control them and their ability to do as they pleased. Sometimes the whole herd had to be stopped and kept rounded up until an obstinate critter could be chased for miles, subdued, and brought back to the herd. The time required to do this depended upon the animal's determination, the power of its endurance, and the nature of the place selected for the contest. If it were on the open prairie, it was only a short job; but if in a thicket, or brush and low timber, where it was not possible to ride a horse with any speed, the animal could browse around indefinitely. Under such circumstances, one would have to dismount and chase the animal on foot; This was where Stogy revealed more than ordinary "horse sense" An ordinary horse would have to be tied to a tree when one left him to chase an animal on foot through the brush, for he would never stand still if untied; and by the time the horse was regained, the stray animal would be back in the brush again. But Stogy did not have to be tied when left. Whenever it was possible, he would follow his master through the brush, and when this was impossible, he would gallop around to the place where the animal was being chased out. I always kept hollering at the animal as I chased him; so Stogy always knew where we were and the direction we were going, and never failed to be ready for use when and where I needed him. When chasing a cow or steer in the open, Stogy delighted in biting it whenever he could make a chance to do so, and he was an expert in this feat. With his bites and my cow whip, the pleasure in straying could usually soon be taken out of an ordinary cow.

Some cattle have a habit of dodging as they are chased. They suddenly wheel to one side, and allow the rider to pass them at full speed. In this way they get some time to rest, for the horse must be stopped, turned around, and another attack made. This wears a horse out while they are resting. But Stogy could and would wheel of his own accord, and do it about as quickly as the animal could dodge. The great difficulty was in staying on him as he made this skillful change in the direction he was going. In time I learned it was best for me to leave the chasing to Stogy, and to make it my business to stay in the saddle.

After a heavy rain one afternoon, Stogy and I went out on the prairie to round up some cattle that had strayed into a herd that did not belong to us. Among these was a steer that preferred to stay with the herd to which he had attached himself, and he was a bad dodger, too. But Stogy was getting the best of him until the steer made a dodge on a "buffalo lick," and Stogy fell as he attempted to stop and wheel around.

In that country there were occasional small spots in the prairies which were called "buffalo licks," because it was thought that on account of grass not growing on them, and there being a saline taste to the oil, buffaloes in earlier times had licked these places to obtain the salt in them. When these spots were wet, they were very slippery, too much so for a horse smooth-shod, as Stogy was, to make a quick wheel, but he attempted it, and every foot went out from under him, and he came down on his side so quickly I did not have time to change my position, and his whole weight came down on my left leg and threw it out of joint at the knee. I could not get up alone, and was in great pain.

Most horses would have run away after they got up, but not humanlike Stogy. He came to me and put his nose down to my face. I clasped his neck and pulled myself up, and in doing so I got my leg in a position that caused it to snap back into place with an audible thud and a sickening pain. I could not move for quite a while, but was able to stand by clinging to Stogy's neck, which he held at an angle suitable to my emergency.

I could not use that leg for anything; hence I could not get up onto Stogy from the ground. But putting my right arm over his neck, and using him as a crutch, and guiding him with my left hand, I hobbled to a near-by ditch, in which I placed Stogy. This ditch was deep enough to bring his back about level with the bank, on which I remained as I guided him into the ditch. It was then possible for me to make my mount, and after finding an easy exit from the ditch, we headed for home without the cattle.

I have often wished that every boy of my age could have had the privilege of observing the looks and the general conduct of that horse from the time he found me after his fall until I left him that night at the door of my home. He gave every evidence that he was ashamed of his fall, and that he was sorry he had hurt me. It made me believe that the Creator made the horse to be, above all other animals, a passive, strong, intelligent companion for man.

Stogy demonstrated many times, and in various ways, that he possessed unusual "horse sense"—sense bordering on human reasoning, which may have been developed in him more than in other horses through his close, intimate, long-continued association in play with all the boys and girls in our neighborhood. Most other horses have only human association in rough, hard, and often abusive labor. Almost any horse is susceptible of culture, some, of course, more than others. This is true even among human beings; some will polish easily, while others seem naturally rusty.

There must be some reasoning power of mechanical intelligence in a horse's mind, when it is not possible to tie an ordinary rope or halter rein so it cannot be untied, in time, by that horse. No boy or man in all our country could tie Stogy so securely with a common hitching rein that he could not untie it when left alone. He never would go about it as long as any one was near him. He would only muss up the strap or rope with his teeth and saliva, but would not cut nor break it, and sooner or later, according to the knot or the combination of knots, he would be loose and visiting around among other hitched horses. He especially resented being tied when other horses were around. He wanted to be friendly—to pass about among them, making and renewing acquaintances. He never made any trouble among them, just quietly nosed around among them. Some horses he seemed to like better than others. If a horse was not congenial, he immediately left him, and found one that was, with which there was considerable nosing, head rubbing, and gentle neck biting.

Neck biting among horses seems to be a reciprocal favor, like, "You scratch my back and I'll scratch yours." If Stogy wanted his neck scratched, he would bite the friendly horse's neck just where he wanted his neck scratched, and the intensity of his bite was the guide for the other horse in the application of his reciprocal bite. That is the way all horses cooperate in all their neck and back scratching.

Often horses have itching collar sores on the top of the neck at the juncture of the neck and the shoulder. While these sores itch intensely when healing, they are tender, and can stand only light biting. In such cases the afflicted horse simply rubs with his nose the other horse at the place of the sore on his own neck, and receives a rub on his sore with the same pressure suggested by the horse having the sore, itching neck. The act of scratching one another is one way horses communicate, and in other acts they talk to each other. All animals have their peculiar ways of communication. It is interesting and edifying to study these animal methods of communication. There are practical moral lessons for man in all of them.

Stogy liked all friendly animals, excepting mules. For them he had only contempt. We could do nothing that seemed to hurt and sour him more than to hook him up with a mule. It was quite a common practice in those days to work a mule and a horse together as a plow team. We soon discovered that Stogy disapproved of this method when he had to be the horse in such a team, so we usually avoided hooking him up with a mule.

He was very fond of colts, and would put himself out to play with them in the same spirit that a good, fatherly man would play with children. He liked dogs and casts. We had a noble shepherd dog I always sent out into the eighty-acre pasture every morning in the summer season to drive in the work horses. Stogy always met him pleasantly, and as a usual thing he would start at once for the barn upon the approach of Shep.

But once in a while he would stage a play with him, pretending he was not going to the barn driven by a dog. On such occasions it was a treat to observe the cunning this noble horse and this wise dog exhibited. To watch them was to convince any boy that animals do plan and reason in animal strategy. But Stogy never kicked at Shep as other horses did, and Shep never attempted to nip Stogy's heels when he playfully refused to go direct to the barn. He seemed to know that it was all in fun.

But when the other horses refused to go, they got a feeling nip on one of their heels, in spite of all they could do. They might run, but Shep could run faster. They might kick, but Shep could dodge kicks by lying so flat on the ground that they could not hit him. Their heels would always go over them, and by the time their feet were on the ground again, they got another nip. And the only defense for them was to run for the barn, to which action Shep offered no resistance.

We had a barn cat that made her living quarters in the barn hayloft, the inside entrance to which was through Stogy's stall. A jump of three and a half feet landed her on top of Stogy's manger, and a jump of four feet more landed her on the loft floor. In cold weather this cat slept on Stogy's fat, warm hips, when he was standing or lying in his warm bed of straw, and he did not seem to object to it at all. In the morning the cat would jump to the loft from Stogy's back; in the evening she would spring from the loft to his back, after calling his attention by a few coaxing mews. Everything seemed to be congenial to each.

But the remarkable thing, for which I relate this instance, is the fact that soon after this cat had three young kittens in the loft, she got one of her legs broken while out of the loft, which rendered her unable to make the necessary jumps to gain the loft. She came around Stogy, hobbling on three legs, and pitifully mewing. Finally Stogy was seen by a farm hand to take this cat in his teeth and lift her to the loft. When this was reported, the cat and the kittens were taken from the loft, and placed where the mother cat could have easy access to her kittens. When the family of kittens were weaned, and the mother cat had recovered the use of her leg, the former relations between her and Stogy were renewed.

Stogy was very fond of shelled oats. But they were high in price in those days, and we fed them very sparingly for that reason. We gave them only occasionally for a change in feed. Stogy always gave a peculiar little half squeal and whinny which I called a laugh, when he saw the oats coming, and he would have his nose in them before I could turn them into his feed trough. We usually grew forty or fifty acres of oats each season, but did not sell them at threshing time, because everybody was selling then, and the price was much lower than at seeding time in the spring. Se we stored our oats in a granary, one side of which formed a side of Stogy's stall in the barn.

Just above his feedbox there was a knothole in a board, but a shingle was nailed over it. But in some way the shingle had worked a little loose. Upon a slight jar of the granary wall in Stogy's stall, a few grains of oats would trickle down into his feed trough. In some way he discovered this fact, and began to dine daily on shelled oats, through the laborious effort of striking the granary wall with one of his forefeet. Until there was a mouthful of oats in his trough. These he would eat, and then pound for more. The sound of his shod foot against the wall could be plainly heard clear up to the house; but whenever any of us went to the barn to try to find the source of the pounding, it ceased. There never was any of this mysterious pounding when any one was in or near the barn.

One day, when Stogy was in the barn, and I was out in the pasture on the opposite side of the barn from his stall, the pounding began, and I quietly slipped up to the barn from the pasture side, and looking through a crack in the side of the barn, I saw Stogy pounding the side of the granary. After he had pounded a little while, I saw him eating something from his trough. I made a noise, and all was quiet inside the barn. I went direct to Stogy's stall to make an investigation, and found that by striking the granary wall a few grains of oats would fall down into Stogy's trough or feedbox. Then upon close examination I found the scars of his feet on the granary wall, and the mystery was solved. I renailed the shingle over the knothole, and got a peck of oats for Stogy, and thereafter I gave him oats every day, for I thought he had earned them. Do you call this performance of Stogy's the product of ordinary "horse sense," or what?

Stogy liked to go to school. The schoolhouse was about two miles from our home, and my two sisters would often ride him to school. We kept him during the day in a comfortable prairie-grass hut built for him in a nearby thicket. He was always in a hurry to get to school, and walk he would not. He insisted on a fast gallop bordering on a run, especially as he neared the schoolhouse, where there were always some children ready to welcome him with their childish exclamations, hand patting, and an apple or two. He was the pet of all the boys and girls, and he plainly showed that he liked it.

At noontime I would take him to water, and one day as I returned from the watering place, I rode him up to the ball ground; and because he wanted to run as he saw the boys run after making a good strike, and all the other boys running here and there, yelling and making a great ado, some one suggested that Stogy run for the batter. That was playfully agreed upon, and I placed him near the batter, headed in the direction to be run, and soon got a good strike to go on, and Stogy made an "I," which meant he went clear around the diamond before he could be crossed out. Several attempts were made to throw the ball between him and the base which he was approaching, but he was too fast for it, and it went behind him each time.

That was interesting to all, but the diamond was too quickly covered by a horse as swift as Stogy, so it was decided to enlarge the diamond, and let Stogy run for all batters. This was so novel and satisfactory that it was continued for a long time, but was finally ruled out by the teacher after several small children narrowly escaped being run over. But while at it, Stogy enjoyed playing ball with the boys.

I loved all of the many horses I had the privilege of associating with on the farm. To this day I frequently dream of them, of going through the pleasant exercises of those happy days with them, but there was something almost human in Stogy that bound me to him with a deep, real affection. I loved him most devotedly, and was weak enough to believe that he loved me as much as I loved him.

On the day I left home to attend Battle Creek College when I was twenty years of age, the last thing I did was to go to the barn and affectionately bid him farewell, believing then it would be only a few months until I should return to him. I said to him,

"Well, Stogy, my dear old pal, I am going away for a while, and I want to say good-bye to you. I wish you could go with me, but I will be back in June."

He did not understand the words I said to him, but he did know the touch and the spirit of my act. I extended my hand, and he promptly gave me his right forefoot, as he always did when I offered my hand, and I patted it and his beautiful neck, rubbed his clean, velvety nose with my cheeks, and finally said "good-bye" for the last time, for I did not get back home for two years, and Stogy died a short time before my return. It seemed to me that a member of the family had passed away.

I Remember

OTHER PET ANIMALS

U PON my return home I went to the barn to look over the other loved horses with which I was on good terms, and found standing before the barnyard gate a large, full-blooded ram which my aunt had purchased at a large price when a little lamb two years before I left for college. He was another special pet of mine. When he was young I played much with him, and taught him, among other things, to butt with me.

Rams fight by butting their heads together. I have seen them rubbing their heads together, seemingly in the most friendly way, when suddenly they would begin to back slowly away from each other, with their heads a little below the level of their backs, and slightly twist them from side to side, and they would continue this process until they were about twenty yards apart, when they would start full speed toward each other, and they never failed to strike each other in a full center, head-to-head, full-power attack. Then they would back off again in the same way for another blow, and keep this up until one of them would acknowledge defeat by breaking away and running among other sheep. I have seen them fight in this fashion until they were completely exhausted, oftentimes with bloody noses and broken horns.

This fighting element seems to be an inborn instinct in all rams. They take it up on the slightest provocation. I thought it was cute in this pet of mine to back up a few feet and run into my fists, when he was only a few months old. My fists were a pretty good bumper for his young, tender head, but his head soon became too hard for my fists; so I adopted the plan of getting down on my knees and hands and backing in this position, and in the charge I would fall to one side just before we came together, thus causing him to miss contact with me. This seemed to satisfy the young pugilist, for he would immediately back up and make another charge, and would keep it up as long as I would play with him. He soon became so formidable I had to change still further my manner of approach. I simply stood on my feet and bent forward and twisted my head back and forth as I backed away from him. It seemed to make no difference to him. In this position I could dodge him quicker and easier just before he reached me. So in this fashion we played together until he was full grown, or until I left for school. He would never offer to play with me until I made the advance by coming in front of him and bending over and wagging my head at him. He would then promptly leave anything he was doing, even at feeding time, and accept my challenge.

As much as I believed in animal memory and power of limited reasoning, I was surprised to find my ram recognized me at once, as was demonstrated by his enthusiastic sheep talk of "Baa! Baa!" licking my hands, and rearing up against me. He closely followed me as I made the rounds of the barn and barnyard, but I did not offer to play with him, because my folks had told me of the nuisance he had become as a result of my having taught him to butt with me. Whenever he saw any person stooping down and twisting or moving in any way while in that position, he regarded it as a challenge for a butting match, and immediately proceeded to accept it.

A neighbor's timberland lay a mile or so beyond our farm. It was nearer for this neighbor to pass through our farm by means of gates; so when he walked to his timber in the winter to split rails, he passed through the gates of our barnyard. The front gate of the yard could be opened without stooping but the gate opening out of the yard into the pasture was fastened by a hooked chain near the bottom of the gate, to prevent the hogs from squeezing through it.

When the neighbor, with ax and maul on his shoulder and iron wedges under his arm, stooped and wiggled about, fumbling with one hand to unhook the chain, the ram saw him, and thought it was a challenge for a knockout. And as he was about the right distance away, he lost no time, but plunged into the neighbor with full force, and knocked him clear through the gate, as the chain was released just at the instant the blow came from the ram. The surprised cry of the neighbor, the rattle of the ax, maul, wedges, and his tin dinner pail on the frozen ground, so startled the farm workers who were in the barn, that they ran out into the barnyard just in time to catch the ram by the horns as he was backing up for another blow. That neighbor never went through that gate again when the ram was anywhere in sight.

That ram gained a neighborhood reputation for his man-butting propensity, acquired when a lamb through the teaching of a boy who then did not know it was unwise to teach even a domestic animal to bestow its brutal powers upon human beings. He enlarged his neighborhood acquaintance by disturbing a religious service one hot, sultry Sunday afternoon.

During the summer season all stock in that section of the country was turned loose on the range. Our flock of sheep especially liked the grass around the old stone church located in the edge of the timbered land about three miles away. There was no fence around the church, and the grass about it was a kind that sheep liked; so they were there or close by all the time.

On this particular Sunday afternoon, many of the flock of sheep were lying in the shade of the church and others were browsing around about the church. The old ram worked around in front of the wide-open door, which was level with the ground. In that door sat a weary farmer, nodding. He was humped over forward, raising and lowering his head as he peacefully nodded. The ram saw him, and evidently thought he was being challenged for a butt, and promptly backed away and plunged, knocking that nodding farmer against the people sitting in the backless seat of the back row of the church. The yell of the nodding farmer, the screams of the women directly involved in the collision, and other noises of the whole affair, created a full-fledged disturbance. The ram did not come back for another butt, for he saw only a lot of confused people making movements, but not of the challenging kind.

As I entered the horse stalls of the barn, in the first double stall the four bright eyes of two black mules beamed upon me. They were the eyes of Jack and Jill, then four years old, the beginning of the prime age of mule life. They were bought by my aunt at weaning time in the fall of 1873. At that time our part of the State was new, and there were but few well-improved farms. Nearly all the water supply for the stock was secured by digging large basins in hard spots of the ground known as "hard pan," and when these were filled with water by the heavy spring and fall rains, they were called ponds.

During the long, hot, dry months of the summer, these ponds often became dry, and as there were no running brooks or constantly running streams in this part of the State, and but very few wells or large standing pools of water in the creeks, stock often suffered severely for water. It was during one of these dry times that Jack and Jill forever settled the question often discussed by us boys in our country debating society, "Resolved, that animals reason."

The water supply on the farm had given out, and all the stock, excepting the hogs and very young or weak animals, were driven once a day to a large pool of water in the bed of a creek three miles away. In the barnyard was a cistern containing an old fashioned wooden pump, with handle and spout, but no trough. This cistern was kept well filled by drawing barrels of water in wagons from the creek, and emptying them into the cistern. This supply was only for the hogs and other animals too young, fat, or weak to travel.

Now, if you can imagine two little jet-black mules, only about two years old, with eyes and entire faces fairly beaming with intelligence, standing at their barn windows close to the pump, and looking wistfully at us boys while we were pumping and carrying

93

water to the hogs a few yards away, you will have a picture of a
daily scene on the farm where Jack and Jill lived.

One day, as we were going to the barn to water the hogs, we
were surprised to find Jack and Jill in possession of the pump,
they having jumped through their open windows. Jack, with his
long ears laid back and his neck stretched straight out, had his
mouth up to the spout of the pump, and was drinking as hard
as he could under the circumstances. Jill, with her forefeet upon
the curb of the cistern, was grasping the handle of the pump
between her teeth, and rapidly raising and lowering her head,
causing the water to flow out of the spout into Jack's mouth,
and, of course, all over the ground.

Sometimes the water came slowly, and then Jack's patience
was tried, and he, keeping his mouth up to the spout, turned his
heels toward Jill, and made a kicking demonstration that she
seemed to understand. At least she made a more vigorous effort

at the lever, and the water gushed over Jack's face, up his nose, and all over the ground.

After a few minutes of faithful labor, Jill seemed to think, "Turn about is fair play," and leaving the lever, she attempted to push Jack's nose away from the spout, but as her nose came close to Jack, he ungratefully bit it, whereupon she wheeled around and pelted Jack's side with her heels several times. Though protesting all the time, Jack finally gave up the spout, and very reluctantly took the lever in his mouth, but gave it only a few strokes, when he attempted to force Jill away from the spout. Her indignation was so aroused that she flew at him with her eyes shining like fire. Though he did all he could to defend himself, she punished him so thoroughly that he seemed to take pleasure in pumping for her until she had finished drinking.

Then Jack jumped to the spout again, but Jill seemed to think he had had his turn the same as she had, and ought to be as well satisfied as she was. Jack, however, was persistent in his demand for more water. Getting on the opposite side of Jill from the pump, he laid back his ears, opened his mouth, and went toward her in as threatening a manner as possible, to drive her to the pump. Then quick as a flash he made for the spout, and putting his mouth to it, looked all kinds of ways at Jill. First he looked coaxingly at her, then with a woebegone expression, ending with a threatening look. When Jill refused and turned to leave the pump, he followed her, kicking and driving her back. This maneuvering was kept up for some time, when Jill finally took the lever again, and pumped until Jack quit drinking.

Then, as they stood there looking at each other and the pump, seemingly congratulating themselves upon their wonderful achievement, we boys, who were hiding behind a fence, sprang out in sight, and throwing our hats into the air, gave three cheers for Jack and Jill, as they went scampering away across the pasture.

These mules continued to pump water for each other in this way as long as the drought continued, the privilege being granted them for the amusement of the neighbors and those who chanced to pass along the adjoining highway.

AFTER THE WAR

FTER the hardships of the Civil War, when everybody had to depend upon himself, it was natural that the habit of strict economy and self-denial would be a marked characteristic in the future lives of all the survivors. They would be pardoned were they to become unduly close. Doubtless many did continue to deprive themselves and their families of much they should have had for health and comfort.

The country people in that new, war-stricken State saw or handled but little money. The raised practically everything they ate. They sweetened everything needing to be sweetened with molasses they made from sugar cane they grew. They made their own coffee of corn, rye, wheat, or peas. Their tea was made from sassafras roots, which grew wild in abundance. They made yeast from their home-grown hop vine. They made fruit flavorings from their own orchards. All meats were from their own herds, and all vegetables and grains from their own fields. All clothing was made from the cotton or flax grown in their own fields, or from the wool grown on their own sheep. Their shoes were homemade from skins of their own tanning, and their corncob pipes were filled from their own tobacco patch. They made their candles from the fat of their own beeves. All their soap was made from the ashes of their own home fires and the fat from their own smokehouses.

Practically everything to eat or to wear was home grown or homespun. So there was little need of money for anything save for the purchase of more land and more stock, for which there was a constant demand. But even in these transactions, little actual cash was handled, for it was largely done through charge and credit accounts.

To illustrate how the young people were impressed with the importance of economy and sacrifice, I will refer to one incident which throws light on the general attitude of that time in the matter of spending money:

One autumn day, accompanied by two sisters, I drove to our town with a fine four-horse team, attached to a new Studebaker wagon loaded with sixty bushels of wheat. There was enough money invested in the team alone to buy one of the best houses and lots in the town. The wheat itself in the wagon was worth $150. Besides, there were several thousand bushels like it back on the farm, ready for the market, and we also had many thousands of dollars invested in stock. In fact, great value was in evidence on every hand, for everything grew into value rapidly after the close of the war. And yet, in the face of all these evident resources, my sisters and I felt conscience-stricken after the three of us had purchased and eaten, as we rode home, ten cents' worth of soda crackers—ten cents spent on ourselves!

We were not accustomed to spending any money upon our selves. It seemed to us wasted, or at least, in our minds, unnecessary outlay. We could have spent a thousand dollars for land or live stock and not felt a twinge of regret or had a though of extravagance, for it would have been money invested and not consumed upon ourselves. Those were days when people sacrificed and invested, and their wealth rapidly increased. They were producers rather than consumers. But today the general tendency is to gratify every personal desire, out of all proportion to the income. The people of this country are rapidly becoming consumers rather than producers.

CHILD CODDLING UNKNOWN

In those days the practice of coddling children was unknown. Parents did not favor themselves, nor spoil their children by encouraging them to give up for every little ache or pain. One evening I was playing tag in the yard with one of my sisters. I was running around the house after her, and stepped on a newly sharpened hoe and cut my foot badly.

The best attention was given to the wound that night by the adult members of the family. But the next morning I found I would be required to plow just the same as before my foot was cut. While it was securely bound up, it was very painful. The wound being on the bottom of the foot, I was sure the hard clods rolling into the furrow would constantly strike it and produce added pain, and perhaps infection. But I *had* to plow! There was no getting around that fact. It was hard on the foot and its owner.

Many were the times I had to stop and writhe in pain when I stepped on a hard clod of dirt or a cornstalk stub. But while it was hard to bear, it was worth a great deal in educating me not to surrender to even more severe handicaps. Today a boy hurt as badly as I was would be hurried off to a hospital in padded ambulance, and after the wound was disinfected, he would be put to bed and kept there for several days. And then, for four to six weeks afterward he would be exempt from all labor. But how would that experience help prepare him to take the real bumps of life courageously?

At one time I had a very large carbuncle on the back of my neck. It was a *real* affliction. Even the jar of careful stepping was enough to make my entire head feel as if it would burst. But I had to plow just the same, for it was seeding time, and help was scarce. Besides, it was *only* a big carbuncle, which would care for itself in time. It was finally opened by a horse throwing his head forcibly around in an effort to stop the biting of a large horsefly as I was adjusting his harness. His nose struck my carbuncle square, and made me see stars. But the carbuncle was opened, and shortly I was greatly relieved. To every boy does not come the thrill of having a horse perform his surgery.

At another time I cut a deep gash clear across my kneecap with a corn cutter. This is one of the worst places for an injury of this nature that can be found on the human body. Though I could not bend my knee for weeks, and seemingly during that time *everything* hit it, I had to continue to cut corn.

My much-loved uncle was an old forty-niner who had gone through enough to kill ten ordinary men, and yet he had learned, through rough knocks, that hardship makes more men than it kills. He gloried in success over difficulties. He was a devout Christian, yet as firm as he was good. I believed implicitly in him. To me, what he said was definitely fixed, and had to be, without any reasoning on my part. And I usually found his ways to be the best in the long run, whether they appeared to be so at the time or not.

To give a glimpse of the general character of this good man, I relate the following experience which came to me when I was seventeen years of age:

It was the custom in those days for neighbor to help neighbor in harvesting and threshing time—"swapping work," we called it. The men would join forces in cutting, threshing, and marketing the wheat and oats of the neighborhood. It came our time to haul our wheat crop to town, seven miles away. It was August and very hot. Everything was dry. Even the *good* wagons seemed to be loose in all their joints; and *old* wagons were at their worst.

To me was assigned my favorite four-horse team and the old wagon of the farm. The harness for these four horses was also quite old, though it did not look dilapidated. But the life in the leather of this harness was practically gone. It could not stand an unusually severe strain. My uncle knew all this better than I did, but he fixed me up with this outfit, loaded the wagon with thirty two-bushel bags of wheat, and started me off ahead of all the other wagons. He told me to take the short road to town, which was one mile less than the long way around, but much rougher. I wondered why uncle wanted me to take the short way, since I drove the first load out, and for that reason would have more time for the trip. But his word was law with me, and I did not question, but struck straight for town by the short cut. I overheard one neighbor say to my uncle as I pulled out, ""That wagon will never get to town over that rough road with sixty bushels of wheat on it." I could not catch my uncle's reply, but I knew by his look there was a question in his mind also.

About two miles from town, on the short-cut road, there was a bad crossing of a wet-weather drain way called 'Blackwater Creek." Of course, it was dry then, but the banks were very steep. I knew there was danger at this place, and I did all that could be done to guard against any possible trouble. But that load of sixty bushels of wheat was too much for that old wagon under the least extra strain. As the front wheels struck the bottom of this ravine, they snapped into pieces with a crash that frightened the horses. They plunged forward against all my effort to hold them back, and stripped themselves of all connection with the wagon, only the lines holding. They dragged me by the lines some distance, but I finally quieted them and tied them to trees until I inspected what was left of the wagon. I found it a complete wreck, in a deep ravine under sixty bushels of wheat. The harness was broken so badly as to be almost beyond repair. What could be done?

I did not know by which road the other teams were coming. And even should they come my way, they could not get past my wrecked wagon. Something must be done at once! I took my lead team and galloped into town. There I visited our well-known hardware merchant, Mr. Bettis, and told him I wanted a new four-inch-skein Studebaker wagon and two full sets of harness, explaining to him my breakdown, and telling him I could not positively assure him that my uncle would approve of the purchase of this new wagon and harness, but that I knew he *needed* a new wagon, and he could see for himself the old harness would require a costly repair job, and then would be only old at best. I simply asked to be allowed to borrow the whole outfit to get my load of wheat to town as quickly as possible. But I suggested to him that when my uncle saw his fine horses in the kind of harness I would select and the new Studebaker wagon shining behind them, it would mean a sale of a good Studebaker wagon and two sets of expensive harness.

He said, "I think you are right, especially under the circumstances. Pick out your harness while the boys grease up a wagon for you."

In a short time I had the team hooked up to as fine a wagon as ever went over the rough roads of Missouri, and they seemed to be proud of the new harness decorating them. In the wagon was another set of harness for the team I left tied to the tree near the wreck. I was soon back at the scene of the accident, and faced the hard job of transferring thirty bags of wheat from deep in the ravine to the new wagon, parked on the bank as close by as possible. I had to carry the bags up a steep fifteen-foot bank. It was a hot, sticky afternoon, and the perspiration flowed freely, but I was anxious to get everything out of the way before any of the other teams came along, should they come that way, and above all to see how my new outfit would look when it was ready to go. And so I rather enjoyed my laborious task.

I was soon ready to attach a long chain I had also borrowed from Mr. Bettis, for the purpose of dragging out the wrecked wagon, which I dumped to one side out of the way of the traffic. Then came the never-to-be-forgotten pleasure of hooking up those four fine big horses, decked out in as good harness as was made in those days, to the acknowledged best and finest looking wagon made. I can feel the thrill of it yet! And the horses seemed to share my pleasure.

The other ten teams drawing my uncle's wheat did not take the short cut, and I had the pleasure of that road all to myself. The other wagons reached town a long time before I finally made my appearance. The men had unloaded and were loitering about the post office and stores, waiting to see me drive in, for the hardware man had told some of them (not my uncle) of my visit to him. My uncle (so they told me later) said he suspected I would have some kind of breakdown, but he wanted to see what I would do in an emergency. Some of the men were anxious to drive out to meet me, and possibly help me out of some difficult place, but he objected, saying, "Wait; I think he will pull in soon."

When they saw me coming some distance away, they reported to my uncle I was coming on a swift trot, making the dust fly. But he was not much concerned until I turned into the street near where he was standing. The horses were champing their new bits, heads up; and the new wagon was musically creaking under its 3,600 pound burden of golden wheat; and I am sure there was *some* pride revealed in *my* general appearance also. My uncle was greatly surprised. His expression was the most peculiar combination of wonderment and pleasure I have ever seen. He calmly said, "What's all this? It seems to be the same horses and the same boy. Is the wheat the same, or is that changed also?"

I replied, "Uncle, the old wagon went all to pieces in Blackwater Creek, and the horses became frightened and literally tore themselves out of the harness. The lines were the only things that did not break. So I saved a runaway through their holding together. I came to town, and Mr. Bettis kindly lent me the new sets of harness and this wagon so I could bring the wheat in." by that time the men about town were all gathered around, looking the outfit over. My uncle calmly climbed up on the new spring seat by my side and had me drive down to the grain elevator, going along to help unload the wheat.

After the load was deposited in the elevator, he directed me to drive up to the hardware store, where he called Mr. Bettis out and told him to charge the price of the harnesses and the wagon and an additional $10 for his favor. Mr. Bettis gave me a pleasant, knowing look, and jokingly said, "How much will it take to buy the boy? Leave the boy, and taketh harnesses and the wagon to even up."

My uncle answered, I do not think the boy would leave this outfit for your whole store. Besides, we need him on the farm."

He then asked one of the neighbors to hold the team until he and I did a little trading. He bought me a fine new hat, a pair of new shoes, and a pair of buckskin driving gloves—the pride of all farmers in those days. Then we all started home-eleven four-horse teams—forty-four as fine horses as ever trotted on the Western prairies. And my four, decked out as they were, followed by the best wagon in that region at that time, and driven by the proudest boy in Missouri, led the caravan.

This episode, which had been deliberately planned by my uncle with others as an educational factor in my life experience, has been of great value to me all through my life. He was willing to risk the wreckage of his old wagon and the injury of at least some of his four good horses, to say nothing of my personal injury, in order to teach me self-reliance and resourcefulness. He purposely put me in a tight place to force the development of these elements which are very necessary in every boy's life. He knew it was best for my future good.

How different the great majority of parents are today in their dealings with their children! The general practice of parents today is to shield their children from trying, testing experiences of every kind, thereby weakening them throughout their entire lives, and robbing them of the pleasure, the essential satisfaction, and the seed planting in character, through the knowledge of having conquered in difficult accomplishments without the aid of others. Good child training includes testing,—hard things to do in physical, mental, and moral life.

THE ACCEPTANCE OF THE MESSAGE

THE acceptance of the teachings of Seventh-day Adventists was by far the greatest of all my experiences. At that time I was completely absorbed in my farm work and the community social affairs. I was not interested in religious things. I attended church regularly, but more from a desire to be in company with the people than to hear the preacher.

Then R. J. Lawrence, from Michigan, came to our neighborhood, and began to preach in our country schoolhouse evenings on the prophecies of the Bible. First our family went occasionally, then became regular attendants. My aunt, who was now a widow, at once believed all he preached on the coming of the Lord, the nature of man, Spiritualism, and health reform, which was her special hobby. But the first evening he preached on the Sabbath question, Aunt made a beeline for him as soon as the meeting closed, and insisted that he go home with us for the night, in order that she might show him from her own Bible that Sunday was "the Lord's day." he accepted her invitation, and we all sat up until after one o'clock that night, waiting for her Scriptural proof of Sunday sacredness. But at last we went to bed, on the promise that she would remain up until she found what she *knew* was in the Bible.

Though Aunt did nothing else for several days but search her Bible for authority for the observance of Sunday, she found only added evidence of the sacredness of the seventh day. This was a great surprise to all of us, but, true to her general nature, as soon as she found no Bible evidence sustaining Sunday, she entered into a thorough study of the entire Sabbath question, and began to keep the seventh day after a few weeks. The rest of us did not join her; so she at once began with her two-meal, cold-water-bath-every-morning intensity to work on the rest of us, in order to bring us to the point of seventh-day observance. But it meant so much in the management of the farm to make such a change that I did not decide to do it until three years later.

Her bachelor son, twenty years my senior, and my two sisters soon joined her in Sabbath observance, but I did not. My cousin was sorely afflicted with asthma, and did not do regular work on the farm anyway, so he could keep the Sabbath without materially affecting work on the farm. But I was the head of all the farm force, and could not see how it was possible, with Sunday-keeping hands, to manage successfully the farm work.

I believed Saturday was the Bible Sabbath, but being unconverted and wholly absorbed in farm work and community social affairs, my heart was more fixed upon them than upon my personal religious obligations. In fact, I had no conception of personal religious responsibility. While I was not an unbeliever nor an atheist to any degree, and not tinctured with bad habits of any kind, my heart was wholly in the things I was then doing, for I thoroughly enjoyed them. Every hour of the life I was then living was full of joy and happiness. I could not see how keeping another day could improve it, but I thought I could see how it would greatly interfere with my work, and my future plans and social relations.

The country was so new and rich, while grain and stock were so scarce and high, it was really fascinating to be prolifically producing and rapidly converting all kinds of grain and stock into multiplied dollars. While the land was as rich as it is possible for land to be, it was low in price. In the fall of one year we added to our farm 160 acres, every foot of which had a four-foot black soil. We paid only $480 for the 160 acres. It lay in the open prairie, unimproved in any way.

That winter, while the teams were not busy making crops and the ground was not frozen, we broke up the sod on this 160 acres and let it rot during the coming summer. In the fall, just one year from the time of its purchase, we sowed it in wheat, without the necessity of replowing. That was all the work done on it until harvest time. It produced the following summer 4,000 bushels of good, hard winter wheat, which we sold for $8,000 in less than two years from the time we bought the land, and had the land left in good shape for future cultivation. Thus a good farm of 160 acres paid for itself in two years, and left enough margin to pay for fencing and all improvements.

Raising stock was also profitable. A farmer gave his sixteen-year-old boy $25 in cash as a reward for his summer's work on the farm. The boy bought five calves that fall, paying $5 each. It cost practically nothing to feed them during a few cold snaps in the two winters he kept them. They were on the range during the long summer season. When the calves were two years old, he sold them for beef at $60 each. They had cost him but little labor and expense, so the outlay of $25 produced $300 in two years.

The same farmer offered to give the same boy a sick pig if he would nurse it through its sickness. He did a good job of it, and inside of four years the boy had sold over $1,000 worth of pork, and besides had 140 breeding sows, and over 1,000 growing pigs all of which would have brought, at the lowest price, $3,600. Thus this boy, without expense to himself, made over $1,000 a year in his hog line alone, and lost no time as a husky farm hand.

But one of the hardest things for a young man or woman to do in accepting the truth at any time is to sever the strong ties of social friendships, especially when the one who is called to give up such relations is a leader in local social affairs. "The tie that binds" the youthful heart is exceedingly strong. It requires a definite conviction of personal obligation, and the power of God, to do it. It involves far more than a mere change of mind.

In my case, I was the principal social leader in our neighborhood. In all our community school exhibitions, and there were many, I was the manager and principal actor; in our winter and summer singing schools, I was the organizer; in our writing schools, I secured the teachers; in our debating societies, I was chief; in all picnics, I was to provide the place and program, in all winter house parties, I was expected to lead; when any of the young, or even old, people were married, there *just had to be* an old-fashioned charivari for them, and I was expected to be the captain of the noisy gang. My charivari propensities, however, ended naturally with the following incident:

Two of my most intimate friends were married on a cold winter day, and I was the best man for the groom, and accompanied the couple from the home of the bride to his home after dark, in order that the charivari party would not know where we were; but we failed, for the largest gang of boys and men ever known to take part in a charivari in that section of the country came down upon us just when we were congratulating ourselves on having outwitted them. After they had demonstrated what a tremendous noise they could make, I went to the front door of the house, and opened it for the purpose of congratulating them, and then to present the bride and the bridegroom, and to pass out the refreshments all charivari parties expected. But just as I stepped in the open door, two double-barreled shotguns were fired just above my head from each side of the door. These guns were only heavily charged with powder, but the concussion so close to my head caused me to drop as if I had been killed. This so frightened the gang that they ran away before any one could recognize any of them. I was only slightly powder burned, but was decidedly stunned by the force of the explosion of so much powder so close to my head. Thus ended the ceremonies of that wedding, and my participation in any way with charivari parties.

But the above narration pertains only to comparatively easy parts of the mercenary and social functions, that were easier for me to give up than my personal fondness for the one expecting to be my life mate. Her only brother and I were inseparable

111

friends for years, before we had any thoughts of, or affection for, girls. We were the same age, and he was the only young man I ever knew with whom I could talk as freely as I could think to myself; and in this free, easy, confiding way we always communicated, no matter what the subject was.

His mother was a well-to-do widow, dependent upon her only son for the managing of her large estate—a strong man's job put on the shoulders of a boy. This responsibility sobered him, and caused him to look upon life in a very serious, practical way. He had heard all the teachings of Elder Lawrence, and believed all he heard, but his mother objected to his keeping the Sabbath. We had freely talked it all over, and decided that sometime we would keep the Sabbath when Anna (his sister) and I, and he and Lou (my sister) were settled in homes of our own. But he died in an epidemic of typhoid fever, and that seemed to bind me the closer to the family.

The winter following the fall of the typhoid fever scourge, in the wee hours of the morning, as Anna and I were driving home from a party held quite a distance from our immediate community, she said, " I heard tonight that you were going to be an Advent."

I asked her to tell me her reply to the report, and she said she promptly told the person that she knew better, for she knew me well enough to know I had too much good sense to throw my life away by joining such an insignificant set of people.

She had heard all I had heard of the teachings of Adventists, and had read all I had read bout the doctrines, and said it was sound. But now it seemed she had no thought of ever trying to live it, and was certain I had no thought of accepting it. But her statement went through me like a piercing arrow and caused me to think seriously for many days.

Up to that time I had made no definite decision about joining the Adventists. I had believed all they taught, but was not planning to join them. The death of her brother, my closest friend, and the influence of her mother had hardened her spiritually, and brought her to the point of rejecting all she formerly believed to be true, and to try to influence me to give it all up.

Her reference to the Adventists' being an insignificant people had some justification, in so far as I was concerned. In fact, there were less than 12,000 of them in the entire world at that time, and we knew of only twenty or thirty, comprising the unorganized body in our community, and most of them were not among the influential people of the neighborhood. And yet this accusation nettled me, for the good sense she credited me with having reminded me of the fact that in religion the majority is always in the wrong, and that in the Bible the promises are always made to the humble, sincere little flock—to those who have kept the commandments of God, which include the Sabbath.

And in addition to all this convincing evidence, I had the present living example of my loved, conscientious, God-fearing aunt, who always followed a "Thus saith the Lord" in all her living. And she was a confirmed Adventist, and in my heart she was not to be classed as "insignificant." The word "insignificant" stung my very soul, and I resented it in burning silence, with the first definite decision that I would, at the earliest possible date, identify myself with this "insignificant" people. The attack upon them came from one who, while mentally assenting to their doctrine, was the means of bringing me to a definite decision, not only to join them, but to sever *all* alliance with worldly-minded people, no matter how dear they might have been. The crisis had suddenly come, and was silently but definitely met in my mind.

This was the most severe sacrifice I had to make in changing the whole course of my life, but it was made soberly, honestly, and, to me, profitably in every way all through life. No matter how favorable everything may appear to be for the union of believers with unbelievers in our message, the Lord has something far better for a conscientious believer than an unbelieving companion.

LEAVING FOR
BATTLE CREEK COLLEGE

THE first of January, 1875, I left the farm for Battle Creek College, little realizing that the move meant farewell to my dearly loved aunt and all her family, as well as the dumb animals, and the beautiful farm I had helped make from virgin soil. It was another great change in my life, a change I might not have made had I known the heartaches that would follow.

I had never been on a passenger train before, though I had for several years longed to ride on one. It was a thrilling time for me. For weeks before the day set for my departure, the thought of being on a passenger train for nearly three days and two nights was enough to obliterate all regrets at leaving home and friends.

But trains then were rude constructions compared with the trains of today. The cars had no closed vestibules and no steps for entering. All depot platforms were built up to the level of the car floor, and all passengers boarded the train from these depot platforms. There were no air brakes in existence then; all trains had to be stopped by hand brakes. A brakeman worked the brakes on the platforms of two adjoining cars. He got his signals from sharp, slightly prolonged whistles of the engine—

two blasts to apply them and one to release them. There was therefore a constant tooting of the whistle, for the roads were not graded as they are today, and brakes had to be applied on all downgrades and released on all upgrades, in addition to all stops.

There were no sleeping cars at that time on Western roads. All the sleeping was done while sitting upright on a springless seat. There were no steel rails on any of the roads, just clumsy, soft iron rails. And there were no clasps binding the rails together at each end, as there are today. And the ties were not placed as close together as they are at the present time. The rails soon flattened at each end, so that there was a bump at the end of each rail, and the rails were only half as long as they are today. The engines were wood burners, with very large flaring-top smokestacks. The cars were heated by wood stoves placed at each end, and lighted by kerosene lamps hung on the walls of the car. Yet for that time they were wonderful, and to me a great delight.

Early in the morning of the day I left home, I found that a number of hogs had broken into the "North 40" of standing corn. I called the dogs, and spent my last hour before leaving, chasing hogs, which was no unusual chore, for hogs from the adjoining prairie had been a constant source of annoyance to us for years. I said to my aunt when I came in from the chase, "There, Aunt, I hope I won't see another hog until I come home, and I hope *you* won't have any by that time."

When I arrived in Battle Creek, I was still asleep, not having been awakened by the brakeman just before the train reach Battle Creek, as he had promised. The train was slowly moving away from the station as he called me. Imagine my surprise and disgust as I ran to the door and jumped straight out from the platform, and lighted in a pen of fat hogs that were waiting at the stockyard for shipment!

I had never jumped from a moving train before, and did not know I should jump in the direction the train was moving. It was fortunate for me the hogs were there, for they were much softer than the hard, frozen ground. But I was tough and used to bumps; so the fall hurt only my pride in the presence of the people who came running to me.

Before I got back to the station, the hacks had all gone and I was left to find my way to the college on foot. I found plenty of good people who put themselves out in giving me all needed information, and I went strolling up Main Street to the Review and Herald Publishing House.

Evidently I was a conspicuous newcomer, judging from the way everybody I met looked at me. While I had no hand baggage identifying me as a traveler, and no overcoat, as all other men had, I had a Missouri hat, a gray suit cut and fitted in Missouri style, an old-time comforter around my neck, and a pair of bright fluffy hand-knit mittens on my hands. My trousers were tight over my heavy boot tops, and rather short for good Michigan style—everything good, but decidedly not the fashion in Michigan.

Out in our community, every one spoke to everybody he met, strangers and all. Every one merely said "Howdy," which was a contraction of "How do you do?" but my aunt said that was not cultured—that it was far better to say "good morning" before noon, and "good evening" after noon. So that was my custom of salutation with everyone I met.

As it was 1. P. M. when I landed in battle Creek, I said "good ev'nin'" to everyone I met. That was something new in Battle Creek, and decidedly amusing to those "Michigan Yankees." It emphasized my peculiar looks. Had I said "good afternoon," it would have been less strange to them. But I did not know anything about "afternoon." With the Missouri people it was always morning from twelve o'clock at night until twelve o'clock noon, and after that time it was evening until twelve o'clock again. We divided the day into only the evening and the morning.

When I reached the Review and Herald, Warren Bacheller, to me a remarkably fine-looking man, was standing in the front entrance of the main building, and while he was looking intently at me I said, "good ev'nin'. Where is the Battle Creek College?" My Missouri drawl and peculiar looks, with my "Good ev'nin'" salutation, at once interested Warren, and he asked me to come in and wait until he finished a job, and then he would take me up to the college. This generous offer was heartily appreciated, and made me feel at home there in the Review and Herald, about which I had heard so much.

I had read the *Review* and the tracts and books that had been printed and sent out form there. I felt that I was in a very sacred place, and this handsome little man was like an angel to me. It was difficult for me to suppress the tears that kept my eyes unpleasantly moist. Everything seemed so large and grand to me. He pointed out our frame church building across the street, which was in real fact a very humble, plain building, but as large as any of the popular churches in my home community upon which I had looked as towers of strength in comparison with our country schoolhouse meeting place. It comforted me in the decision I had made to leave these large Sunday-worshiping churches, and cast my lot with a people who kept the Sabbath, and who also had a large church like theirs.

He pointed out the beautiful new college building, set in a well-kept, beautiful grove of oak trees with grass; and the sanitarium just across the street from the college building, then only a large dwelling house with a two-story frame "L" built on for treatment rooms. It was also set in a large grove.

To me it was all wonderful, and greatly strengthened my courage, which had begun to wane a bit after leaving Chicago, on account of my weariness and seeing only small, sandy soil truck farms—a country that looked to me too poor to raise black-eyed peas—and the people becoming more and more reclusive and less sociable. The towns were all right, excepting that almost all the back yards were dirty and decorated with small chicken coops and pens containing only one or two hogs. All of this looked primitive and shiftless to me. To say the least, I did not like the country nor the general cast of the people.

The job Brother Bacheller had to finish before he could leave to take me up to the college, was finishing printing the last form of that week's *Review*. He had only a few more impressions to make before the job was completed. He was the fireman and pressman for the one small Cottrell and Babcock cylinder press the house then had. It was run by steam generated in a small wood-burning boiler located in a room to the right of the press-room and six feet lower than the pressroom. He would feed the press as long as there was steam enough to make it go, and then stop it altogether and go down and fire up. He would have to wait a while after filling up the boiler furnace with wood, until sufficient steam had accumulated to operate the press. It was during his waiting period that I came along, as he was standing in the front door, and saluted him by saying, "Good ev'nin'."

While I was waiting, Brother George Amadon, who was foreman in the type room, came down to complain about a "work-up," and Brother Bacheller asked him if he could take another student boarder and introduced me. Brother Amadon said that if I would room with Mrs. Amadon's nephew, W. B. White, he could take me for $2.50 a week, which seemed to me like a big sum to pay for just staying there. I had not been used to paying anything in money for board and room. But I promptly accepted, without revealing my mental conception of the price. They hooked up the office horse, and at once took me down to the railway station to claim my trunk, and I was soon established in my pleasant new home.

It was a surprise to me when I was told that the school was not held in the new college building, because the night before the steam pipes had frozen up, and repairs could not be made before the spring term—that the school would be continued in the Review and Herald building for the winter term.

It was an unusually cold winter in Michigan, but to me it was the most comfortable winter I had ever passed through, because I did not have to be out in the cold except on the way to and from school, and the Eastern homes were so snugly built and comfortably heated I did not feel the cold as much as I did in Missouri. It seemed to me, however, I was doing wrong in having such a comfortable time and paying out such a lot of money for it.

I was delighted to find so many students in the school as old as I was, and even older, and no farther advanced in their studies. The college had gathered in many of our young people form different States, who had been deprived of school privileges during the Civil War, and for some years after the war, on account of the scarcity of labor and the general strenuousness of the times—those who desired to fit themselves for some part in connection with the heralding of the message. It even seemed strange to me to see heavily bearded men going to school, and in classes with boys and girls in their teens; but I soon became accustomed to it, and all got along together in splendid Christian congeniality.

The majority of those attending Battle Creek College at that time found places in the work as soon as they could assume them. Some had to leave school before they wanted to, in order to fill some urgent calls.

The teachers with whom I came in contact when entering the college were prof. Sidney Brownsberger, Prof. G. H. Bell, and Miss Nellie Wheeler, who later married Dr. Will Fairfield. There were other teachers in the lower grades, among whom were Mary Ann Davis, sister to W. K. Kellogg's first wife, and later chief secretary of Mrs. E. G. White; and Mrs. Emma Woolsey, the widow of a prominent contractor in Battle Creek.

When the school opened in the fall following, Miss Jennie Sprague and Miss Nellie Rankin were added to the faculty. While I admired all these teachers, in my fancy, Miss Rankin was a queen among them all. I was in none of her classes, but her general bearing in all her work was perfect, according to my judgment of womanhood. Later came Prof. Julian Spicer, brother of Elder W. A. Spicer, who taught Greek, Latin, and higher mathematics. It was thought by all students that he was the best-educated teacher in the school. There was no question in the mind of any who knew him but that he was as honest and sincere a Christian as could be found anywhere. I was in his Greek classes for two years, and greatly admired him in every way.

There were a number of part-time teachers. First among these were Elder Uriah Smith, whose Bible teaching embodied all the doctrines taught by the denomination, and Dr. J. H. Kellogg, then a young graduate from Ann Arbor. He taught physiology and gave lectures on various health topics. Later other teachers were employed, but these I have mentioned were the only ones present at the time I entered the school, and to all of them I owe a great debt of gratitude. They were all firm believers in the old-time, simple message that had called me from the farm and planted in my heart a desire to do all in my power to deliver it to others.

They were really hardworking people, teaching every hour from 8 A.M. until 4 P.M., and often had extra students in the evening. They received very low wages for long, hard work. The tuition was exceedingly low. I bought a three-year scholarship for $30, only $10 a year, and this included some of the higher grades. My first six months in Battle Creek College cost me less than one hundred dollars.

School opened at 8 A.M. and closed at 4 P.M., with one hour for dinner from twelve to one. Our only business was going to school. Some of the students, however, worked for private parties from 4 to 6 P.M., and from 5 to 7 A.M., but most of them had to study all the time they were out of school, with the exception of the time spent in preparing their food and caring for their rooms, which, I assure you, did not consume much of their time; for the food was exceedingly plain, cheap, and not always properly prepared. As a general thing, two students roomed together. Often the rooms of the two-boy habitation were not very attractive, to say the least. Such a den would not be tolerated today. And yet such boys grew fat in flesh, and surprisingly bright in their schoolwork.

The two-meal system was the universal custom in those days among our people everywhere, and rigidly adhered to by our Battle Creek students. Judging form what I observed as I visited the rooming places of the boys, the old-fashioned oatmeal mush and Graham crackers always constituted the breakfast menu. This old-time oatmeal had to be cooked a long time, so in the evening, as the boys studied, the oatmeal for breakfast was on the stove, filling the room with the familiar odor. I used to declare I could tell an old-time Battle Creek student in the dark, because he emitted a pronounced identifying oatmeal odor.

Dried apples and prunes were also staples in the students' diet, not because they were extra good, but because they were cheap, and could be cooked by the slow process on the back of the evening stove (the only time there was fire sufficient to cook in the room, and could be watched through the study hours. Plain boiled potatoes were also a staple in the student menu, for they were cheap. Bought direct from the farm wagons, they cost only twenty-five cents a bushel. The navy beans were also very cheap, and extra good in Michigan. Baked apples were as good as they were cheap, and milk was only four cents a quart.

The usual student price for a single room was fifty cents a week, crudely furnished with an old cook stove or a combined cook-and-heating affair, usually unpolished; an old-fashioned slat bed and straw tick (the students had to provide their own straw, at ten cents per tick, cash and carry); old-time quilts; washstand, washbowl, and pitcher; wood-bottomed chairs; coal oil lamp; wood box back of the stove; no carpet, often no window curtains; no shades, only the outside blinds; no dishes; no toilet; no bath. The cost of food per person averaged about fifty cents a week.

Laundry expenses were very slight—for boys, especially, because they wore plain shirts with detachable celluloid bosoms, and washed their collars and cuffs, also their shirts, handkerchiefs, socks, and underclothes, every week in their washbowls. Among the boys, Sundays were washdays, except that the celluloids were washed on Friday, in preparation for the Sabbath. They usually had no change in this part of their wearing apparel, for celluloid can be washed and dried immediately. Washdays added materially to the frightfulness of the boy-student room, for poorly washed wet clothes hung everywhere, to be dried by the heat of the stove.

To our college boys of today, such surroundings and such food as I have described in my portrayal will seem simply horrible; but after all, it was not so bad to us as it sounds today, for we were not accustomed then to the luxuries we have today. Nobody lived then as people do today. No one had *rugs* at that time. Floor coverings then, when used at all, covered the entire plain unfinished wide-board floors, tacked down tight all round close to the baseboard, with straw under them to hold the carpet off the floor, and to allow dirt to settle beneath the straw.

Most floor coverings then were hand woven, regular rag carpets. Those who had factory-made, ingrain carpets, were as proud of them as people today are over their expensive Oriental rugs, and the few who had Brussels carpets were regarded as aristocrats. Carpets and coarse-tanned and mud-polluted boots do not belong together at any time. Refined things belong together, but I wonder whether real refinement in the lives of people today has kept up with the elegance of living.

While the early Battle Creek College students had no elegantly furnished rooms and no fine clothes, their behavior in every way and everywhere was far more refined than their homes and their clothes, and they found that beautiful clothes, elegantly furnished rooms, and luxurious food were not necessary to the rapid accumulation of knowledge.

The girl students in the early days of the Battle Creek College fared much better in every way than the boy students, because they were good cooks, natural homekeepers, and all of them could make their own clothes, which cannot be said of all girl-student bodies today. In keeping with the times, it was more necessary for girls to do all these things then than it is to-day. But the fact is the girls of those days could outclass the boys economically in every way. Perhaps they can still do so. But after all is said and done, it did not seem to be in keeping with the nature of young men to be long enslaved by the custom of only two of them secluding themselves the monotony of such small units.

THE BEGINNING OF DENOMINATIONAL BOARDING SCHOOLS

A T THE time Battle Creek College took possession of is first new buildings, January, 1875, the student body boarded in private families at a standard price of $2.50 a week, or rented rooms and boarded themselves. These two methods were generally followed until the establishment of the Student's Boarding Club in 1877, which developed into the Welch Boarding Club in 1878. This club boarding place came into existence through a chain of circumstances forcing its establishment.

At the opening of the fall term in 1877 six young men rented three very plainly furnished rooms and opened a bachelor's hall. The personnel of this group was as follows: J. T. Richards, L. T. Nicola, I. J. Hankins, Joseph Smith, Harry Rue, and D. W. Reavis.

The three rooms these young men rented had no floor covering of any kind. One room as furnished with an old-fashioned, corded bedstead and straw tick; two straight, wood-bottomed chairs; washstand with washbowl and pitcher. In another was a plain kitchen table and an old, worn-out cook-stove. The third boasted a lamp stand holding a kerosene lamp, a small sheet-iron heating stove, and a bed.

Each one of us purchased his own few pieces of chinaware, spoons, and a steel knife and fork. We agreed that two were to get breakfast, two to get dinner, and two to wash dishes after each of our two meals. Other work, such as buying the provisions, splitting and bringing in wood, carrying water, and special baking, was assigned individually. It was an economical arrangement, and in every way more pleasant than any other plan we had tried.

At the beginning of this term of school these six young men became members of Dr. J. H. Kellogg's physiology class, and he at once began an experiment with them, because they were good physical specimens and living together and boarding themselves. He put them on a limited diet of one pound of cooked food for each meal—two meals a day, only *two pounds* of cooked food a day!

He afterward said the allowance was to have been one pound of *uncooked* food at a meal, but we all maintained that he definitely specified *cooked* food. The test was to be very rigid and exacting. There could be no violations in weight of the food or in frequency of meals without a fine of 25 cents for each offense. There was to be no eating between meals of any kind. Not even gum chewing was allowed.

Just over our dining table, we suspended from the ceiling a spring scale, with a wire plate holder. We placed our plates in this holder, and then put on just the additional pound of whatever food we had to eat. Weighing the food was a very entertaining part of the meal, for all were interested in seeing that each one had only his pound. A pound of cooked grains or vegetables does not bulk large. It looks very small to a robust, hungry youth, but small as it was, it was the limit allowed. No liquids were used, because of their heavy weight and small nutritive value. The food tasted so good and was so limited it was thoroughly Fletcherized, not from principle, but to prolong the pleasure of tasting. That in itself was a great advantage.

But all of us were hungry *all the time* from September to January, the period of the test, hungry even when we finished eating. The only time we were not conscious of hunger was when asleep, and even then we often dreamed of good things to eat. As we went back and forth from our rooms to attend classes, we had to pass through an apple orchard, in the midst of which stood the new college building. In the fall these vigorous apple trees were loaded and the ground was covered with the most delicious Northern Spies I ever saw.

Imagine the temptation this luscious fruit would be to healthy young fellows who were limited to two meals a day, and only one pound of cooked food at each meal! But as far as my knowledge goes, there were no transgressions, with the exception of one instance. One cold, crisp afternoon when we came in from school, the sanitarium bakery had just delivered to our buyer a barrel of fresh, broken Graham crackers. They were yet warm. They proved to be *too* tempting! For the first and only time during the test we yielded to temptation. We did it deliberately and openly. All of us paid our fines in advance. And then! Such crackers! There was no question but that each ate a quarter's worth.

At the end of the term, nearly four months in duration, all of us were in good health and maintaining usual weight. None of us had been sick during the time, even with a headache or a cold. All got the highest averages in grades. In fact, everything was favorable to the test, with one exception of a constant, unappeased appetite.

Four months of intense fasting brought us to consider seriously the whole question of more desirable and yet economical culinary arrangements. So during the holiday vacation, when the stringency of schoolwork was temporarily removed, arrangements were made with Mrs. Welch, a widow with a family of four grown children, to prepare, cook, and serve in her home all of our food. We were to buy the food for her week by week, and pay her 50 cents each for service. We organized ourselves into a Boarding Club, appointing one of our number as buyer and treasurer, and then went out among other young men students who were boarding themselves, and invited them to join the club.

At the beginning there were sixteen members. The total cost to each member the first week was 90 cents—40 cents for the raw food and 50 cents for service. This rate was maintained for a long time—until a more liberal menu was demanded. And even then, the cost was only about $1 a week; and the board, while plain, was good enough for anybody.

At any rate, it was good enough to tempt some of the young women students, who at first had not been interested in our project. We now opened our doors to them, and in a short time there were as many women as men availing themselves of the privileges of the club. It was found to be much better for the students in every way than the old plan of each cooking his own food.

The students continued to conduct this Boarding Club for some time and maintained a low average cost per week, even when it began to grow into a rooming as well as boarding enterprise. Finally the original six became too busy to look after the ever-increasing business, and they prevailed upon the Welch family to take it and run it on the same general plan, allowing additional charges above the cost of food for rent and help. On this basis the Welch family faithfully conducted the club for several years, and served the students, as well as the college, in a very acceptable, economical way.

When the managers of the Battle Creek College decided to build a dormitory for lady students, arrangements were made in this new building for boarding all students, and the Welch Boarding Club, left without patronage, closed its doors, after having rendered valuable service to hundreds of young people.

Besides, it had served to demonstrate the advantages of the boarding-rooming plan, and was largely responsible for the idea of the dormitory and boarding principles then introduced into our denominational schoolwork.

THE PROCTOR SYSTEM

MIDNIGHT oil was common in most students' rooms at that time. They had no young people's meetings, no parties, no special meetings of any kind, excepting a literary society for men and one for women, but neither boys nor girls could attend these meetings together, excepting on special occasions, when everybody in the church could attend. The association of boy and girl students was rigidly forbidden throughout the school year. There were no provisions made for their being together at any time; they were to be absolutely separated at all times. But even then, with a very conscientious, loyal student body, this was a difficult rule to enforce. It is wonderful how infatuations can develop even in isolation.

Clandestine meetings and outskirt strolls became so frequent that the faculty appointed proctors to discover and report the offenders. This seemed to make the situation worse, for while many were apprehended and disciplined, others seemed to enjoy pitting their wits against those of the proctors, and went out on strolls for no other purpose than to confuse the proctors, who were themselves only students with a commission to spy on other students. Things went from bad to worse. Proctors were disliked by all other students, even by those who were 100 percent loyal. It would not have been so bad had all the proctors themselves been loyal to the rules. Some, while spying on others, violated the rules themselves.

One of the most relentless of the proctors was a big, heavy-set German who, while a student, taught a large class in German. He was what we called a student teacher, and was very much liked by all students, until he became a very enthusiastic proctor. He seemed to find much pleasure in discovering transgressors and reporting them. One of his preferred victims discovered that he was most frequently apprehended in a certain neighborhood near the home of the proctor's best girl friend. So he made it his business to spy on the proctor, and caught him so perfectly, there could be no question about it.

Not being an appointed proctor, he could not report the student teacher to the faculty, but he could, and did, report his discovery to a group of boys as they were entering the college campus from Sanitarium Avenue the next morning. It was great news. Other boys joined the party, and the story was repeated to each newcomer until more than twenty boys were gathered, when the offending proctor himself came along on his way to the college. And he was hailed with jeers and accusations that filled him with indignation.

He grabbed the boy who had spied on him, and was just ready to throw him into an open water main ditch filled half full of snow and dirty water, when he was over powered by as many of the other boys as could get hold of him, and he went into the ditch flat on his back and out of sight in the water and snow. He was a sight as he climbed out alone. No assistance was offered him by any of the boys. He was wearing a long, heavy buffalo fur overcoat, a very fine coat in those days, but it did not look fine as he laboriously pulled himself out of the ditch. The only thing he said as he slowly walked away toward his room was, "Of course, you boys will pay for my clothes." it was all done so quickly, and without being planned, no one thought of what might follow. Nothing was said, and nothing happened, but there were no more student proctors.

As a general thing, all students attended all meetings in the church. The prayer and social meetings of the church were held regularly Sabbath afternoons, and more than half of the attendants were students during the school part of the year. The Sabbath school was almost entirely managed by the college, professor Bell being superintendent for many years. And he was just as insistent upon perfect lessons in the Sabbath school as he was in the college.

The only difference in the two schools was in what the pupils studied, and the way they recited. In the weekday school, all lessons excepting reading had to be passed in in written form, and they were marked according to accuracy, penmanship, spelling, form, capitalization, punctuation, and their general relation to the Bell laws of syntax; while in Sabbath school every member had to be able to give a detailed synopsis, not only of the lesson of the day, but of every lesson studied from the beginning of the book (all Sabbath school lessons were then in graded book form, and were written by Professor Bell himself), and do it promptly and vigorously, whenever called upon in class or in general review. And in those days we had reviews often. Professor Bell believed in reviews of lessons in day school and in Sabbath school, and he believed in having the students give these reviews, and not for some one to do it for them. It was a real Sabbath school in Bible study.

When I entered the Sabbath school in Battle Creek, the first Sabbath I was there, Professor Bell personally assigned me to the small class of C. H. Jones, then an enthusiastic young man working in the Review and Herald office. The members of this class were all young men, students. I at once began to invite other students to join our class, and we soon had a class of eight. Then Professor Bell said it was too large, and took out two. I soon had eight men in the class again, and Professor Bell came around and took out four. That was somewhat discouraging, and I asked the professor why he took out so many. He looked at me, and as he stroked his long beard, asked, "Did you not have bees on your farm?"

"Yes, Professor Bell."

"Did you ever rob them?"

"Yes, Professor, often."

"Did robbing them hurt the bees?"

"Not that I could discover."

"Did they soon fill up the hive with more honey?"

"Indeed, they did."

"Is the lesson plain to you?"

"Yes, Professor, I see the point. I will get four more boys to join our class next Sabbath." But the robbing of the class continued.

The second year I was in the class, Brother Jones was called to take charge of the Pacific Press Publishing House in Oakland, California, and I was appointed teacher of the class. But the robbing of the class continued until all student recruits were exhausted, and I had to go to the Review and Herald employees for new members. It was not long until I had a class made up exclusively of Review and Herald men and boys.

The third year I was made secretary of the Sabbath school, which meant that I belonged exclusively to Professor Bell for more than a year, for his Sabbath school secretary was not by any means merely an office holder or an ornament, but a constant hard worker. At an appointed hour Sabbath afternoon I had to go to his home and spend from two to three hours in getting ready for the next Sabbath, including his suggestions as to how he wanted the next session of the school reported, the studying of the lessons for each department, the changes he ordered, faults corrected, and every detail committed to me to have in order before the coming Sabbath.

The following Friday evening, after the ringing of the Tabernacle sundown bell, I was to make my way to the home of Professor Bell to report on my allotted work, and to read to him the report I had prepared for the school the next day. This he would pick to pieces unmercifully at times, so much so that I would have to rewrite it entirely after getting back to my room at a late hour. At times this seemed to be trying, and not necessary, but afterward I found it to be of great value to me, and have been very thankful for it all through life.

Professor Bell always knew what his secretary was going to report, and just how he was going to do it. He also knew that all in the church were going to hear it without any effort on their part, for his secretary was thoroughly trained in the manner of delivery. It had to be fully up to the Bell standard. While I was secretary of the Sabbath school, the church moved into the new "Dime Tabernacle," and I had the honor of giving the first Sabbath school report in that highly prized and largest church in the denomination at that time.

The Tabernacle was in those days called "the Dime Tabernacle," because in arranging for the money with which to erect the building, the method was adopted of having each member pay a dime each month for a year, making a total of $1.20 per member. While I was serving as tentmaster for Elder George I. Butler, a letter came from Elder James White, announcing the plan and asking the cooperation of Elder Butler in putting it into effect. Elder Butler at once called his tent company together, and suggested that we put in $1.20 each and forward it to Elder White. We did this, and had the pleasure later of hearing from Elder White to the effect that the total of the tent company's donation was the first payment in full of the assignment on the Tabernacle. This we all felt was a compliment.

Many of our people gave more than ten cents a month. Some of them gave as high as an outright donation of $100. Mrs. Reavis herself put in $50 cash, and donated an organ, which was immediately sold for $60, making her total donation $110. The Tabernacle was therefore called for some time the

Dime Tabernacle, and finally it was abbreviated to just the word "Tabernacle."

I Remember

OUT OF A JOB—OUT OF SCHOOL

WHEN I left home in January, 1875, the plan was for me to return the following June to take charge of the harvesting of eighty acres of wheat I had put in the preceding fall. That fall the grasshoppers came too late to do as much damage as they did when their young hatched out in May the following spring. Then they ate up every green thing. The ground was left as bare as a rock, and they had complete sway until a very heavy rain and hailstorm killed them off about the last of June.

The farmers then replanted their corn and sowed millet for hay. The corn planted so late did not entirely mature, but was sufficient to make good feed, so after all, the farmers had feed for their stock the following winter. But their wheat and oat crops were a complete loss.

Under these circumstances, there was nothing for me to go home for, and no money for the next year in school, for my cousin was depending on the wheat crop to supply all financial needs, and it had gone down the necks of the grasshoppers. I was, therefore, stranded in Battle Creek, with no money and no job.

I was only a Missouri farmer. While I did not like the looks of Michigan farms, I decided to try to get a job on one, anyway. I struck out up near Lansing, where I was told the best farms were. I started out on Monday morning among the farmers, and was refused employment nearly all the forenoon. I was a real tramp, in that I had no home, no job, no money.

About eleven o'clock, I came to a farm that looked pretty good to me, and as the owner was hitching affine-looking horse to a new buggy in the barnyard, I approached him and told him I was looking for a job. I shall never forget the expression of his face as he looked at me and said, "You looking for work on a farm? Look at your hands! They look like a girl's hands! I don't believe you have ever done a day's work on a farm in all your life. What have you got up your sleeves anyway?"

I replied, "Only a good pair of arms, aching for a job." I briefly told him the facts. He said he was sorry, but had no work before harvest time, which was two weeks in the future. He was a stock buyer, and most of his farm was sown to grass. He said if I would come around at harvest time, he would give me a trial. Then he was ready to go. I asked him if I might saw wood awhile. He had a large pile of old fence rails, evidently intended for wood, and a bucksaw and ax, and a little other evidence of a start having been made on the pile of rails.

He said, "Oh, you need not get all het up sawing wood. go on hunting a job. Perhaps my neighbor over there can help you out. He hires help frequently."

But I did not like the looks of that neighbor's farm; so I stayed anyway, and sawed rails into stovewood until the farmer

142

returned that evening. I had no dinner, but it seemed refreshing to be doing something. When five o'clock came, I asked the farmer's young wife if I cold not bring the cows from the pasture and do the milking. She smilingly consented, and when I brought in the milk, she said it was more than her husband got. (I was accustomed to milking.) I also brought up the horses and fed them, and put everything about the barn in shipshape for the night. Then they invited me in to supper and to stay overnight.

Before they were up the next morning, I had the milking done, the stock all fed, and was sawing wood. After breakfast the farmer said, "If you want to stay with us until harvest time, I will keep you at the rate of $16 a month, and pay you harvest wages all through haying, oat, and wheat harvest." I stayed, and after harvest was done, he paid me $25 a month until school time, and then begged me not to go back to school, but to stay on his farm indefinitely. But I went back to school at the opening of the fall term, with money enough to pay all my expenses for the full school year.

I Remember

MY FIRST EXPERIENCE AS A
TENT MASTER

A T THE close of the second year of school, I went back to Missouri to be tent master for Elder J. G. Wood, grandfather to Prof. L. H. Wood, and stayed to teach a country school the following winter.

Elder Wood conducted two tent efforts that summer, one in Appleton City and another in a small prairie village near Nevada City. He began the last effort Friday night, and announced a meeting for Saturday night, with D. W. Reavis, a student of Battle Creek College, Michigan, as speaker. Subject: The Great Prophecy of the Bible Recorded in the Second Chapter of the Book of Daniel.

It was to be my first sermon, and it weighed heavily upon my mind. I was in very deep water in every way. I knew my subject, for I had studied it more than any other part of the Bible. My Bible was well worn all through that book and the Revelation, for in those days Adventists spent much time on these two books of the Bible. But a weight of heavy responsibility, dread, and fear came upon me. It was a most serious thing to me, but a great relief came when a severe storm blew our tent down about four o'clock the next afternoon, apparently too late for it to be put up and in shape for meeting that night.

But Elder Wood was determined to have a meeting, and we worked hard to get the tent up. I told Elder Wood that if he did have a meeting, he would have to do the speaking, for certainly I could not be prepared to do it under the circumstances. Never before nor since have I been compelled to work hard upon a job I did not want to see completed. I felt the Lord did not want me to be the speaker that night, else He would not have permitted the tent to be blown down. I felt that He was displeased with the whole affair! And I was more confirmed in my belief when we were just ready to raise the tent a half hour before meeting time, and found the main tackle block at the top of the center pole had been split when the tent fell, and would not bear the weight of the wet tent, so the tent could not be raised that night.

But among the crowd that had assembled on the tent lot was the teacher of the village public school, and he told Elder Wood he was welcome to use the schoolhouse, which stood less than a hundred feet away. That favor was not appreciated by me, but the elder and the people thought it was a happy solution of the situation. So I had to get out the tent lamps and fix them for the schoolhouse. Some of them had been broken in the collapse of the tent. I had to go some distance to the village store to get chimneys for all of them.

By the time the schoolhouse was ready for meeting purposes, it was fifteen minutes past the appointed hour, and I felt pretty blue, for I had had no time to pull myself together through a rehearsal of my speech, nor even a moment alone with the Lord, who I was sure was unwilling I should present that subject to that people, and I begged Elder Wood to let me off that once. But he said the people had come to hear me , and it would be against our work there if I disappointed them. He said he would make proper explanation for my not having time to get my lecture better in hand, and he would open the meeting and be right on the stand to pick up the subject just where I left off, and complete it; for me to go ahead and take the prophecy as far as I could, and stop whenever I felt like it. That nettled me, and I resolved to tell all I knew about the kingdoms included in the prophecy of the great image of Daniel 2, if it took me all night, and to do it with all the fire there was in me.

Well, it took me just one and one-half hours, talking at full speed, to cover the subject, and then Elder Wood had only to apologize for the long service. He had no fear after that about my running out of something to talk about, and said I had amply qualified for a Seventh-day Adventist preacher, in so far as pertained to the length of a sermon.

I Remember

MY SECOND SEASON IN TENT WORK

THE next summer I accepted a call to serve Elder George I. Butler as tent master in a strong tent effort to be made that season in Sedalia, Missouri, a large railroad center. The business was not entirely new to me, because of the previous year's experience in the same kind of work in small towns. The city phase of the work, however, had to be learned.

At that time Elder Butler was president of the Iowa Conference, president of the Missouri Conference, and also the only speaker in this large tent effort. He preached every night, and wrote out his sermons by hand the next day for a chain of daily papers throughout the States of Missouri and Texas. His tent company consisted, in addition to himself, of Elder Hollenbeck, a blind musician, who played the organ and sang solos; John McReynolds, a Bible worker and valet for Hollenbeck; and myself—tent master, cook, policeman, and general manager, ready to do everything needing to be done.

Our new 50 x 70 foot tent was located in the very heart of the business part of the city, where a speculative farmer was holding about one acre of ground as an investment. The lot faced on three of the principal streets. High billboards had been erected on these three street fronts of the lot, but they had been blown down. We piled them neatly along the closed side of the lot back of the family tent pitched as sleeping quarters for the preacher and the musician, and also to serve the company as a kitchen and dining room. McReynolds and I slept in the large tent, he because there was no other place for him, and I because I was needed there every night to keep out prowlers and often to keep the tent from blowing down. I assure you the wind knows how to blow in Missouri! Frequently it was necessary for me to be up all night, tightening the ropes before the rain came and loosening them after it began to fall. I have ever been proud of the fact that the tent never blew down under my care.

I had good rich soil hauled to the lot, and filled all holes and low places; then I sowed Bermuda grass seed. This grass is a quick-growing, blue-stemmed, tough grass, and it was soon up enough to make the entire lot look inviting. It thrives on abuse. With our clean, new tents, decorated with plants and flowers, the place was attractive enough to tempt many of the business-men of that part of the city to spend a part of their noon hour with us.

Soon after our meetings began, Barnum's Circus was booked for Sedalia, and early one rainy morning, the city billposters came to replace the billboards around our lot. I objected, for putting these boards around our lot and having them covered with circus pictures meant ruin to our meetings. In those days tents were only associated with shows. Our tent enclosed with billboards covered with circus pictures would have attracted on-ly the undesirable element, and placed us in an environment out of keeping with our work.

Knowing the character of a large number of people ever present in our Western railroad centers, I had, when we first came, qualified for regular police work by applying for and securing an appointment as special policeman. I wore my police badge on my coat lapel, because I soon found out it could do more toward keeping order about the place than I could do personally.

So when I told the leader of the billboard gang he could not replace those billboards around our tents, he said he would have to report my decision to his boss and await further orders. When he left to report the decision of the special police, I went to the small tent to tell Elder Butler what was happening, and to learn just what kind of contract he had on the lot. I found he had only the owner's verbal consent that we might use the lot for meeting purposes. No definite time was covered by this permission. It could have ended at any hour of any day. I proposed that he go out to see the farmer at once, and secure from him the exclusive use of the lot for a definite time. Elder Butler sprang to his feet at my suggestion, seized his rubber raincoat, stuck his trousers in the tops of his high rubber boots, and struck out through wet cornfields to the farmer's house, which was two miles distant as the crow flies and three by road.

He found the farmer in his barn, and soon had his signed lease of the lot until November of that year. A few minutes later the owner of the billposting business drove up. He knew Elder Butler, and at once said, "Well, Elder, if you have beat me to it, get into the buggy and ride back to the city with me, for it is a very unpleasant day for walking." he brought Elder Butler clear to the tent door, and asked me if he could remove the old billboards we had piled up in the back yard.

This instance is related to show the general make-up of that doughty old veteran, George I. Butler. He never hesitated to go after things he wanted, and he usually got what he went after. He did not refer important business to others. He attended to it himself.

As a special policeman, I did not find it necessary to magnify the office at all. I had the confidence and the full cooperation of the police department. The influence of that department was back of me in keeping good order in and around our tent lot. While there were many rough characters in the railroad shops, in only a few instances was it necessary to use my police authority. The knowledge of my *being* a policeman was sufficient to command order.

While my principal position was that of tent master, I did many other things. My tent was kept conspicuously clean and in good order, always ready for the appointed services at least an hour before the time the meetings were to begin, for I was usher during the time the people were arriving. I always met each attendant and made him or her feel at home. I also had charge of the singing and the formal opening of each service. This included the taking up of all the collections, making announcements, the sale and distribution of literature, advertising, etc. Every day when the weather was favorable,—when no storms were brewing and the wind was quiet,—and there was some other member of the company free to stay with the tent, I went out calling, and solicited the aid of young people in our song services. I would go through the shops, greeting the men with their smoke-covered faces, and inviting them to come to the tent early to help us sing. They could not sing very well, but it did them good to *try* to sing, and they appreciated the invitation, and were usually present and did their very best.

We had no one to stand up in front and beat the exact time and conduct a singing drill, but everybody sang and seemingly enjoyed it. The people said they liked to come to the tent because it was so cozy and cool, and because they had such a lovely time singing together. There is such a thing as worshiping *the act* of singing instead of worshiping *through* singing.

After the meetings were well started, I usually had to go to some church each Sunday to report an opposition sermon, for all the ministers of the city were vigorously opposing Elder Butler. In the beginning Elder Butler seemed to be proud of the fact that he had a shorthand reporter. At least he took pains to let it be known. In his first review of an opposition sermon he stressed the fact that he had in shorthand the very words of the speaker, and there could be no going back on what he had said. Shorthand was a new thing in those days. There were but very few who could write it, let alone report.

I was also the all-round business agent of the tent company, buying all supplies and repairing all breakages. I was cook, dishwasher, and housekeeper. We bought large wild black-berries at ten cents a gallon, and other small fruits at about the same rate; watermelons as large as one could carry cost ten cents, and the old-fashioned muskmelons were five cents to ten cents each. The milkman who passed our lot many times a day gave us all the milk we wanted. A bakery near by gave us all the bread we could eat. The ladies attending the meetings kept us well supplied with pies and cakes. A friendly farmer brought us all the butter and eggs we could possibly use. When we wanted vegetables, all I had to do was to make it known to the many ladies who constantly vied with each other in cooking them for us. In fact, we had so much to eat I was always glad when a tramp came along to help us out and we fed a lot of them. It was seemingly a part of our gospel work.

So being cook for the company really meant principally providing the food rather than preparing it. And, confidentially, I found it much easier to provide it than to prepare it. Also, my boarders suggested I could do a better job providing than preparing food. Well, at any rate, I managed the tent cafeteria. And it *was* a cafeteria, for every one had to help himself. But I did *really* wash the dishes.

After a few weeks, when the novelty had worn off, the attendance at our meetings fell off a little. There were a number of interested people coming regularly. But Elder Butler liked the inspiration of large audiences. So he told me I would have to get the people back in some way. I proposed posting the city with a large announcement posted on the sidewalks, which was then a new, novel way of displaying advertising, and allowable by law in the city of Sedalia. The walks then were all made of dressed boards to which ads could be easily and securely posted. The elder questioned this, but finally gave his approval. The method being settled, the next question was the subject to be advertised. Elder Butler had succeeded in other places in reviving declining interests by preaching a sermon on the personality of Satan. So he told me to get up a good ad on that subject. I wrote up one something like the following, and had it printed in display with much large wooden type, on a sheet of paper 2 1/2 x 3 feet in *size*:

"The Devil. Is there a personal Devil? Some say there is and some say there is not. What does the Bible say about it? At the tent tonight, Pearl and Main Sts., Elder George I. Butler will give the Bible story of the Devil—where he came from, his work, and his end. All welcome. Seats free."

I took the posters, with help enough to carry them and the paste outfit, and systematically pasted them at intervals on the principal sidewalks of the entire city. As I finished the work on the far side of the city and was making my way back to the tent, crossing many of the streets I had worked, I discovered the work some bright, mischievous boys had done on one of the posters. They had evidently followed us as closely as possible without being discovered, and before the paste had time to dry, they had cut out parts and rearranged the poster to suit their fancy. They did some clever work. The first neatly readjusted poster read as follows:

"Elder George I. Butler, the Devil, at the tent tonight. Pearl and Main Sts. Seats free."

I thought perhaps only one of the posters had been thus mutilated. But in crossing other streets, I found the work had been general. The next poster I found read as follows:

"The devil at the tent tonight. Pearl and Main Sts. Seats free. All are welcome."

155

Still another read:

"Elder George I. Butler will give the Devil his work and end at the tent tonight. Seats free."

In going over the route to see how extensive the mutilation was, I found all manner of make-ups, and that the boys had done a thorough job of it.

I thought we were ruined. I had never felt quite so bad over the apparent failure of a job I had attempted as I did over that job of advertising. I went back to the tent and freely expressed my disappointment to Elder Butler, and he evidently felt as bad as I did. We had long faces until about an hour before time for the meeting to begin when the people began literally to pour in. The tent was soon packed, and then the lot was filled, and then all the three surrounding streets were literally packed solid with people trying to get as near the tent as possible.

I went down to police headquarters and asked the chief of police to give me assistance, explaining to him how the people were crowding in, and he laughed and said, "No wonder! Any body advertising the way you did might expect just such things." And then he detailed six policemen to help us handle the crowd that night, and the seven of us had all we could possibly do. The interest never waned from that time until the close of our meetings late that fall.

Never will I forget the day the circus was in town. Early in the morning people began coming in to attend the show. Seeing our tents, they took them to be at least a part of the circus, maybe side show tents. I was kept busy explaining to them and directing them where they wished to go. That night after the circus closed, was, however, our worst time, for we were driving away hoodlums till dawn.

Early next morning, not having slept a minute all night, I went out to the small tent to get my preachers up for an early breakfast. I found the door untied. That looked suspicious to me, for I had personally tied it up snugly the night before from the outside. I cautiously pulled aside the loosened door and peeped in. Imagine my surprise to see *three* men instead of *two* peacefully sleeping in the one bed—two clean, innocent preachers with a big, dirty, drunken tramp lying between them. I stood and looked in amazement for some time, trying to figure it all out. I shall never forget the picture! In a way it was pathetic, and a good representation of the mission of the King of Peace to fallen men. Somehow I was moved with compassion for the tramp. I did not feel disposed to be harsh with him, but to befriend him. So I walked in and touched him. He was like a log, just as all benumbed consciences are to the appeal of God, I thought.

Elder Hollenbeck, our blind musician, being a light sleeper, awoke with a start, for he had fallen asleep under a severe strain. When the tramp came in, he thought it was I, and spoke to him. The tramp answered in a mumbling, drunken manner, and the smell of beer filled Elder Hollenbeck's sensitive nostrils. Then he spoke up louder and asked, "Brother Reavis, is that you?" And the tramp mumbled, with all the characteristics of the language of the drunken, "yes, it's me." That was a shock to the good man, and he asked, "Where have you been?" "To—to—to circus!" "What are you going to do now?" "I am going to bed," was the reply. And with that the tramp lay down heavily right upon his questioner, as he occupied the front side of the bed. Finally he rolled over into the middle. Elder Butler did not awaken, so soundly did he sleep.

The tramp was soon in the clutches of a dead-drunken slumber, but my friend Hollenbeck lay there amid the nauseating fumes of liquor in great distress of mind. "Horrible, unthinkable situation!" he thought. "What can be done to save disgrace coming upon the meetings?" For it was clear to him that I had shamefully fallen, and doubtless some of the congregation had seen me in that condition and would use it against the work. He thought of how they would have to send me home, and wondered whom they could get to take my place.

Thus he worried until completely exhausted, for he was a very sensitive, nervous man even under ordinary conditions. It was no wonder, then, that he awoke when I spoke in attempting to arouse the tramp. Elder Butler was also awakened, finally, when I drew the drunken visitor out of the bed. He was for my locking up the tramp at once, but it was not in my heart to add to his cup of bitterness.

I put some sandwiches and cake in his pockets, gave him my personal card, and led him off to the freight yards, where I knew I could find a friendly conductor whose local freight train would soon leave for the town to which the circus had gone the night before. And through the favor of this conductor, who attended our meetings, this highly privileged tramp had a boxcar ride to the town he desired to reach.

The Sedalia tent effort closed in September with a conference camp meeting held on the fairgrounds, and a church of sixty members was organized. From this church several strong workers came, who, in turn, built up churches and the general work in both this and foreign fields.

I returned to Battle Creek College that fall, having been greatly benefited by the two seasons in tent work and one winter's discipline in school teaching. It was all of greater value to me than the same length of time spent in college. I recommend stopping school for a year or two and engaging in tent or school work, because it gives one a mental and spiritual poise that cannot be so perfectly acquired in any other way.

I Remember

MY RETURN TO BATTLE CREEK COLLEGE

WHEN I returned to college, I found many changes in the student body and in the faculty. New teachers had come into the school, and some of the older students had left school to take responsibilities in the conferences to which they belonged. Among these were Elder and Mrs. Robert Fulton, Elder Henry Nicola, Elder O. A. Olsen, Elder Eugene Farnsworth, Elder R. A. Underwood, Elder R. F. Andrews, Elder A. O. Burril, Elder Andrew Brorsen, Elder E. H. Gates, Elder W. H. Anderson, Elder George O. States, Elder F. D. Starr, Elder I. N. Williams, and others whose names I do not recall. But all were called to important positions in the field, and their sacrificing efforts in the building up of the denomination have become well known. A biography of each of these pioneers, as well as of many others who later followed them through the portals of Battle Creek College in its early days, should be written for the encouragement of the generations following them, for they were all called of the Lord to do a definite work in a special message to the world, and they were faithful to that call. Great will be their reward.

In the main, the students coming to the college at this time were younger than those who had come at the opening of the school in the new college building. But they were not all as thoroughly established in the message as were the earlier students. Some of them needed careful personal help in proper Christian living while away from home. They were in an exhilarating environment, to which they were not accustomed. So Professor Brownsberger selected five young men and five young women, and organized them into a missionary band to do private personal missionary work with selected students. He made himself president of the band, and I was chosen as working leader of the band. The band was to have weekly meetings for counsel, and to report work done and to receive new appointments of other individuals for whom work was to be done. The band was to report to the president once a month.

It was all to be strictly private; no one outside of the members of the band was to know of the existence of such a band or of individuals being labored for. This was to prevent those for whom we were laboring from knowing they were being singled out as those who needed special help.

The members of the band soon found that the work they were doing was as helpful to them as it was to those for whom work was being done, for not only were their efforts appreciated by those in whom special interest was manifested, but this service for others greatly added to their own personal spirituality and thereby to their popularity among all students and teachers. It proved to be far superior to the old proctor method in securing conformity with all school regulations. Many of the students helped through this private, personal work became strong, effective personal workers themselves, for they knew by experience the value of friendly counsel from associate fellow students.

It would be a master stroke if in some practical way every student in our schools could be made definitely responsible for the spiritual good of every individual in the school. The only rule needed in such a school would be, *"Do Right."*

The last two years in Battle Creek College were the busiest years of my life, not alone in college work, which, of course, was greatly increased, but because of the many local interests which seemed to come to me. The Battle Creek church had gradually assumed the habit of depending upon the college students for help in many ways.

At this time the church asked me to supply leaders for eight of the sixteen prayer meeting districts into which the church had been recently divided for prayer meetings on Wednesday evenings, and to keep them supplied through the school year. I was asked to saw, split, and store the wood for the widows and for the rooming girl students, and in the spring to plant and cultivate the gardens of more than a dozen widows, and to attend to many other things that came up from time to time.

I was not expected to do all this work myself, but I was to see that it was done by students. It all took time and strong persuasive powers to accomplish. It could not have been done at all had not the students been willing to do all in their power at all times. The missionary spirit actuated the early students of Battle Creek College. They were always ready to minister to the needs of others in every way.

The girls were no less active than the boys. They found much to do in the homes of poor people. It was not uncommon for them to stay out of school several days at a time to nurse some sick mother. A day out was nothing. Washings, ironings, and sewing of all kinds were common demands upon the girl students.

But in many cases this work freely donated by students was not without its immediate temporal rewards, for those for whom it was done, appreciated it *so* heartily that they found ways to recompense the generous students—a bag of appetizing cookies, a large, delicious, mother-like apple pie, the socks of the boys darned, shirts and underclothing mended, buttons sewed on, coats bound (it was common in those days to bind coats and vests when the edges became worn).

Some of the girls received invitations to spend their vacations, with pay, in another city or on a farm, with well-to-do relatives who had sons from whom the girls later selected husbands. Occasionally one of the boys found that a widow most needy in temporal things had unusual treasures in the form of a daughter for whom he would be willing to work the remainder of his life, and when school was finished, he took her home with him.

One of the boys, who was passionately fond of good horses, was passing a doctor's home one day, and saw a young lady having some difficulty in getting a spirited team hooked to a buggy. He offered his services. He found the doctor was sick, and offered to take care of the horses until he recovered. After the doctor was well, the student seemed to find plenty to do about the place. He continued his missionary work until the doctor gave him his daughter.

After being five years in school work, and working for almost nothing two seasons in tent work, my finances were becoming depleted, and it was necessary for me to find something to do that had some rewards in a financial way. Having had some experience in tonsorial work, I established and ran the first sanitarium barbershop, which was set up in the lounge of the men's bathroom of the Battle Creek Sanitarium. It was open from 4 to 9 P.M. every day excepting Friday, every evening after the Sabbath until ten o'clock, and all day Sunday, which was my busy day. At that time every lady patient had to have her hair cut off, shingled, for the attendants had not then learned how to give hydrotherapy treatments to ladies with long hair. Short hair was compulsory—no getting around it. Many were the fine ladies who burst into tears as I made the first clip into their beautiful tresses. It was always a painful task, although I was allowed 75 cents for each lady.

Only once during the two years I operated the shop did I refuse to cut a woman's hair. It was the hair of the wife of Professor Ramsey, a college teacher. She had a heavy head of most beautiful black hair that touched the floor as she stood. She got in the chair, with the tears freely flowing form her eyes. I silently combed her hair out and tied it in strands necessary for cutting in the longest possible bunches. But when I was ready to begin cutting, I told Mrs. Ramsey that if her hair had to be cut, some other person would have to do it, for I positively refused to do it. She thanked me, and I untied the strands and dressed her hair in her usual style, and she went home happy, and her hair was tolerated in the ladies' treatment room because the barber said it would be sinful to cut such a head of hair, and the nurses were sympathetic in the matter. After that, if a lady patient refused to have her hair cut, she was not forced. Ways were found to give treatment to those having long hair.

Shingled hair for women became quite popular in Battle Creek during the time the sanitarium required all lady patients to have their hair shingled. Many women who were not patients wore short hair.

Outside customers were permitted to have work done in the sanitarium barbershop, provided they were quiet and orderly in the shop; so I had a large student patronage, because they were given a special rate. Many of the poor boys got free haircuts, if they did not come too often, which was the tendency when they knew it was free. I had to shave men in their beds, and all men who died. Undertakers do that work now, but they did not then.

At that time, Professor Hamill, owner of the Chicago School of Oratory, visited Battle Creek College upon the invitation of Prof. E. B. Miller, the teacher of elocution in the college. Professor Hamill was regarded as the best teacher of elocution at that time, and he was given a hearty welcome by our people in Battle Creek. At that time our people were giving much attention to public speaking and reading. A large majority of our preachers had come from the trades and farms, and greatly needed help in the art of delivery. The public conception of proper public speaking at that time was much different from what it is today. Then what was said had to be embellished with speaker mannerisms and acquired oratory, embodying the application of the appropriate quality of the voice, gesture, respiration, articulation, form of voice, force, stress, pitch, and movement. And Professor Hamill knew just how to apply these supposed necessary qualifications to all susceptible pupils. Of course, none of us acquired perfection, but we did our best, and paid Professor Hamill a lot of good money at $1 an hour for each private lesson.

About this time the young men's literary society boasted of fifty *Fide de Lectian* members, most of whom had taken private lessons of Professor Hamill, and were thought to be good speakers. Whenever an open session was held, there was a full house, for the people liked to hear these fiery young men debate.

On one of these occasions the subject to be debated was, "*Resolved*, That the Ancients Were Superior to the Moderns in the Arts and Sciences." On the affirmative were E. J. Waggoner and O. A. Johnson, students in the classical course; on the negative were L. T. Nicola and D. W. Reavis, students in the special English course. After the invocation and society songs, the entertaining feature of this open session was a display of the application of parliamentary rules in the transaction of the routine business of the society. Much was made of parliamentary rules in those early days. Elder Uriah Smith had published a ready-reference chart on the relation of parliamentary rules, and it was standard in all denominational business meetings. Elder Smith was acting that night as moderator, and George W. Caviness as chairman. All the proceedings were full of vigor, and so rapid that the good people of the audience were amazed, and applauded heartily every victory gained through the skillful use of parliamentary rules.

The debate was vigorous, but necessarily dry at first, on account of the nature of the subject. Each speaker had five minutes to present his facts, and the leader of each side had three minutes to sum up his points. The congregation were to be the judges. The affirmative made a masterly showing, but it was all dry, ancient history, in contrast with the negative, facts known to every one present. Yet the affirmative speakers were so scholarly in all they presented, that Nicola whispered to me that we were beaten unless we could make the people laugh. So when he came to sum up his arguments, he used only one minute in actual summary work, and then resorted to witticisms in contrasting ancient and modern arts, and made the people laugh several times, which so pleased him he ran away with himself in the enthusiastic statement, "Why! Down here in Chicago one man can kill, skin, cook, and eat a hog in a minute." That brought the house down, and they laughed and applauded vigorously for some time. Nicola sat down in the midst of it, and the vote, immediately taken, was unanimous in favor of the negative. Just because the people voted laughing.

PROF. G. H. BELL,
A GREAT DISCIPLINARIAN

B Y MANY of the students in Battle Creek College, professor Bell was regarded as a severe disciplinarian, a far too stern one in their judgment; but in view of the fact that he had a conglomerate student body, the great majority of whom were full-grown men and women from socially neglected places, who had acquired a horse decorum, even severe discipline was necessary if reforms were to be achieved, for some were so calloused in their ways that a mere hint or suggestion was not sufficient to work any change in them. In fact, the whole spirit of the entire denomination at that time was reformatory in every detail of life. Strict rules and regulations were established, and all were required to adhere to them without question, if they were to be members in good standing.

Discipline in the Review and Herald, in the Sanitarium, and in the church, was far more rigid than it is today in our churches and in our institutions.

Professor "Bell was no more severe in his discipline than he was required to be under the existing circumstances. To him, through his thorough, hard work, many of the best early workers in the message owe their success. He was an all-round, thorough educator, especially fitted to lay the foundations of our educational work.

While most disciplinarians stress certain features in their work, Professor Bell was the most complete, all-round teacher of order and general decorum I ever met. Yet even he had his hobbies. He wrote me when he learned I had taken a hard school, and gave me much-appreciated counsel upon successful teaching. He did not wait for me to ask for his suggestions. He proffered them. He said he considered the entire life of his students as an exemplification of his work, of which he was very jealous; that the success of his students was his success, and their failure his failure. Among the many excellent things he *commanded* me to carry out was, first of all, order, with thoroughness and promptness in every detail. These were his keystones, reinforced with all the other strength-aiding regulations necessary to being a master in successful educational work.

I had been the recipient of his application of these requirements, and had seen them applied to many others for more than three years. I could fill a good-sized book with the narration of experiences in connection with the Bell system of discipline, but I will give only one.

The name of each member of all classes was written on a separate card, and a class number given to that member, which number was the same in all classes to which the member belonged. My class number in Battle Creek College all the time I was there was 150. Each teacher had a student secretary, or general assistant, who called the numbers on these cards in recitations. When a question was asked by the teacher, the secretary called a number. No member ever knew when his or her number would be called, but all who had been long in Professor Bell's classes did know that the instant the number was called, its owner was to be on his or her feet and the answer given promptly.

Dan T. Jones, who later became secretary of the General Conference, and a life missionary in Mexico, was a schoolmate of mine in boyhood days. He began to keep the Sabbath the year after I left for college. He was the brightest student in our country school, but of a very deliberate nature. He moved slowly, spoke with moderation, and reached all of his conclusions after careful thinking. He was a good Missourian in every way, but grammar and rhetoric were his most difficult studies. All other branches he seemed to understand with but little study.

He had been in the college only a short time, but long enough to try the patience of Professor Bell in our rhetoric class. He always sat next to me in this class. One day his number was called when he evidently was not expecting it. He was to read quite a long paragraph from the textbook, which was cited in the question. He began to hunt deliberately for that paragraph before he made any move toward getting on his feet. Professor Bell could not tolerate such behavior any longer, and he said, "Mr. Jones is evidently asleep. Some one please awaken him."

Dan said apologetically, without making any effort to get up, "No, sir; I am not asleep. I am hunting the paragraph."

Then Professor Bell tartly replied, "Hunting! Hunting!! Do

people in Missouri hunt sitting down? Are you too weak to get up? Boost him, Brother Reavis, boost him!"

All of the class looked serious, but I just laughed. My laughing seemingly hurt Dan as much as the professor's sarcastic reproof, and later I had a hard job erasing my offense. But he got over the affair after a time, and materially profited by the experience.

Professor Bell's advice in the matter of discipline in the tough school I had taken proved to be effective in subduing a rough element that had made serious trouble for a long time, and had finally resulted in running the last teacher out before the term was half through, and the directors could not get any one to attempt to finish the term. There were three Sabbath keeping families in the district, with children of school age, and one of the three directors, all of whom were prosperous famers, was a Sabbath keeper. They told me all about the previous troubles in this school, and begged me to take it.

I had no teacher's certificate, and the only time set for teachers' examination was on the Sabbath. I wrote the county superintendent, and explained why I could not take the examination at the appointed time. He wrote me to come to the county seat sometime before the opening of the school I was to teach.

Meantime we moved our tent so far away it was not possible for me to take an examination before the opening of the school, and our tent season did not close until the Sunday night before the opening of the school the following Monday morning, seventy miles away. Ten of these miles were to be made by wagon, loaded with the tent and its fixtures, which had to be taken down after meeting Sunday night, and delivered that night in the railroad town where I took a night train that put me in a small village three miles from my school at 7 A.M. I was at the school-house in time to open at eight o'clock, after being up all night, with no time for breakfast.

During the Christmas holidays, one of the directors took me up to the county seat, thirty miles away, to see about a certificate. I found the county commissioner to be a lawyer. He had a case in the county court that day, with only one hour between the time I came in his office and the time set for the trial. And besides, he was not quite ready for the trial, that would run all through the remainder of the day, and maybe longer. But he said, "I have heard about your work, that the patrons, even including the conquered tribes, like you, all saying you are the best teacher they ever had, and I know you are a conscientious Christian, because you would not take your examination on the day you believe is the Bible Sabbath. So, I will just ask you a few questions on the branches I know you will have to teach in that school." Within twenty minutes he gave me a high rating and a two-year certificate, and said if I wanted to teach in the county later, he would give me a regular examination upon special appointment.

After it was all over, and as I was leaving, he asked me what I would have done had he for any reason refused to give me a certificate. I promptly replied I would have finished the term.

"But," he said, "you could not have drawn any pay from the county without a certificate, for you had no authority to teach."

173

I said, "I had the authority of the directors at first, and now I have the authority of all the people in the district; and as far as pay is concerned, I have it now in the form of the satisfaction of taming one of the worst schools in Bates County." He said he would like to employ me to tame other tough schools in other counties. One of my two sisters succeeded me in this school, and successfully taught it for two years, until she was married.

Three years later the city school board of Butler, the county seat where I first got my teacher's certificate, offered me the principalship of the public schools of that place. The offer came while I was teaching elocution to the teacher of elocution in the Butler Academy, with a large class comprising the public school teachers of Butler, the Baptist minister, and some of the business and professional men and women of the town.

I was making too much money teaching elocution to consider the wages of the ordinary schoolman. Besides, my burden was not that of teaching school. My purpose was to find a place in the work of God. At that time I needed money, and was getting it faster in elocution work than I could in teaching school. My average income then was $20 a day, which continued, however, only a short time, for a scourge of diphtheria broke out in that section of the State, and I was quarantined in Nevada City for about six weeks. When I got out, I took a train for Battle Creek, and have not pursued elocution from that time to the present.

IN FIELD SABBATH SCHOOL WORK

IN THE judgment of the General Conference Executive Committee, the Ohio Conference needed reorganization of its churches, and it made Elder D. M. Canright president of that conference in the spring of 1879. He asked the Battle Creek College to recommend some one who could go into that conference, reorganize its Sabbath schools, and put in present-used, up-to-date methods, with all our latest Sabbath school supplies. Later Elder Canright came to me and informed me that I had been recommended to him for Sabbath school work in Ohio, and asked me to spend my summer vacation in that work in the Ohio Conference.

At that time there were no conference nor General Conference Sabbath school organizations. There were, therefore no conference Sabbath school secretaries, nor was there a General Conference Sabbath school secretary.

I found each Sabbath school in Ohio conducting its affairs in its own way; and looking back from our present developments, those ways look exceedingly primitive. Most of them had no Sabbath school supplies at all, not even the lesson books, and no records of any kind. They were simply reading selected chapters of the Bible, and commenting on them as they read. In some places they had merely memory verse recitations by the

175

children. Some churches had no Sabbath schools at all.

The work assigned to me was to organize the Sabbath schools in the conference, and equip them with lesson books for each department; class records, which at that time made record not only of attendance, but of scholarship according to recitation; secretarial record books; songbooks ("Song Anchor" then); and to teach them how to use all these supplies.

Elder Canright toured the conference two weeks ahead of me, setting the churches in order along all lines except the Sabbath schools, to which special line I was assigned. He paved the way for me in every possible way, especially admonishing the churches to comply heartily with all I should suggest in their Sabbath school work. He was a fine general to follow, providing one was able to do all he left to be done. But while he left much to do, he left the churches hungry for help, and that was a great aid in accomplishing some things I found necessary, to assure improvement in the Sabbath schools.

Nearly all the schools had antiquated superintendents, whose conceptions of a Sabbath school were not at all modern, and never could be changed. The only thing to do to improve the school was to change the superintendent, and to surround the new appointee with a good secretary and the best possible teachers. All this was a hard task to perform without hurting the feelings of any. With one exception it was done in every church in the conference, and that one offended church, or certain individuals in it, became resigned before our general Sabbath school convention held in connection with the camp meeting the following September. The Sabbath school work in Ohio has prospered from that time forward, and that conference has the honor of having had a conference Sabbath school secretary, without his being known as such, before such an official was known by the denomination.

In my travels in Ohio, I had a very narrow escape in another fall from a moving train. I was to change trains at a junction station, but on the train on which I was traveling was a delegation of ladies who desired to have a train-stop visit with another delegation of ladies at the station where I was to change trains. I seemed to be the only person to get off or on the train at this small junction station, but before I could get my two heavy packages of books to the car door, the platforms and steps were packed with women who were greeting a crowd of women standing close to the train on the station platform.

I tried in a reasonably mannered way to get through this gay, noisy jam, but made little headway before the train began to move out. The stop was a very short one, anyway. I made all possible speed, but the train was moving quite rapidly when I reached the lower step of the car. I was wearing smoked glasses, which made objects appear closer than they were. The platform of the station seemed to be only a few inches lower than the car step, but really it was much lower.

My heavy packages of books added to my hard fall on the platform; I fell on them and rolled off the platform, which was about eighteen inches higher than the railroad track, which was less than two feet away from the platform. Every one seeing me fall thought I had rolled under the wheels of the passing train, but fortunately (I believed providentially) I landed compactly, close to the side of the platform, and was not touched by the train. But I was touched enough in other ways without the touch of the train, for my clothes were badly torn, and I was bruised all over.

But out of it all I got a new suite of clothes and a needed surgical operation. I had been suffering for more than a week with a boil, or something worse, in my right ear. Whatever this was, it affected both of my eyes, making them very sensitive to light, and constantly giving me great pain. I had never had a doctor, and did not take time to see one now. The bump I got in my fall opened whatever it was in my head, and gave me the first relief from a sickening headache I had had for a week, and I had no more eye trouble. But the breaking of this thing in my ear gave me the appearance of being severely injured. My books were scattered everywhere. But I was soon intact and ready for my train when it pulled in about an hour later, and I spoke that night to an audience on the second coming of Christ, an appointment Elder Canright had made for me two weeks before.

I found Elder D. M. Canright, who was then regarded as one of most efficient ministers, to be a most congenial man, fair, honest, ready to help everybody in every way possible. He was a wonderful help to me, and I shall always feel greatly indebted to him.

My summer's experience in the Sabbath school work in the churches of the Ohio Conference was very pleasant, and highly profitable to me. It made my last year in college easier, and in every was more enjoyable.

ELDER D. M. CANRIGHT

WHATEVER Elder Canright said and wrote in those days meant as much to our people as the words of our most prominent leaders do today. But in view of what he has said and written since that time and because of my intimate association with him, I feel it to be my duty to make a brief statement, with all the love in my heart it is possible for a human being to have for an admired, fallen friend.

I was acquainted with the Canright family during his first marriage, his first wire, who died in the faith, being a close friend of some of my intimate friends, and I felt highly honored by being selected by Elder Canright to do special Sabbath school work in Ohio. This appointment proved to be the beginning of a very close, mutual, friendly association.

Elder Canright talked freely with me about everything in which he was interested, about his personal difficulties, about his past trials and sorrows, and of his future hopes and plans. He seemed to find consolation in going over these things with me. He evidently felt that while I sympathetically listened, I would not repeat. Not until the present have I made any public statement of the facts I am now to state, and these are given not to condemn him, but, if possible, to save others even as strong

179

as he from the pitfall into which he fell.

His estrangement began and developed through harboring that greatest seductive thing that finds its way into some human hearts, which I name *an abnormal desire to be great*, not great in the true meaning of the word, but great only in the estimation of people—to be popular.

The elder was remarkably bright, and grew rapidly from his humble beginning, through the blessing of God, and the power of the message he proclaimed with Heaven-bestowed ability. He was so greatly admired and openly praised by our workers and the laity, that he finally reached the conclusion he had inherent ability—that the message he was proclaiming was a hindrance to him rather than the exclusive source of his power. He gradually grew sensitive and resentful, and when reproof came through the testimonies, he rejected it, and finally gave up everything and began warring against the Spirit of prophecy and the message which had made him all he was.

During the summer and fall of 1880, immediately after graduation, I, with other students from Battle Creek College, attended professor Hamill's School of Oratory in Chicago. Elder Canright , inoculated, at heart, with a belief that through a thorough study in, and mastery of, expression he could accomplish his consuming desire to be a popular public speaker, joined us; and because of my former pleasant association with him, I became his critic as he lectured, upon invitation, through the influence of the School of Oratory, in many of the largest popular churches in Chicago during the summer vacation of the pastors of these churches. In these lectures he applied the oratorical principles taught in the school, and needed a critic versed in these principles, to follow him in his lectures and later point out his misapplications, and of course to compliment him on all that were rightly applied. He had more invitations than he could possibly accept; so he selected the largest and most popular churches.

One Sunday night, in the largest church of the West Side, he spoke on "The Saints' Inheritance" to more than 3,000 people, and I took a seat in the gallery directly in front of him, to see every gesture and to hear every tone, form of voice, emphasis, stress, and pitch, and all the rest. But that was as far as I got in my part of the service, for he so quickly and eloquently launched into this, his favorite theme, that I, with the entire congregation, became entirely absorbed in the Biblical facts he was so convincingly presenting. I never thought of anything else until he had finished.

After the benediction I could not get to him for more than half an hour, because of the many people crowding around him, complimenting and thanking him for his masterly discourse. On all sides I could hear people saying it was the most wonderful sermon they had ever heard. I knew it was not the oratorical manner of the delivery, but the Bible truth clearly and feelingly presented, that had appealed to the people—it was the power in that timely message. It made a deep. Lasting impression upon my mind. I saw that the power was all in the truth, and not in the speaker.

After a long time we were alone, and we went into a beautiful city park just across the street, which was almost deserted

181

because of the late hour of the night, and sat down to talk the occasion over and for me to deliver my criticisms. But I had none for the elder. I frankly confessed that I became so completely carried away with that soul-inspiring Biblical subject I did not think once of the oratorical rules he was applying in its presentation. The we sat in silence for some time. Suddenly the elder sprang to his feet and said, "D. W., I believe I could become a great man were it not for our unpopular message."

I made no immediate reply, for I was shocked to hear a great preacher make such a statement; to think of the message, for which I had given up the world, in the estimation of its leading minister, being inferior to, and in the way of, the progress of men, was almost paralyzing. Then I got up and stepped in front of the elder and said with much feeling, "D. M., the message made you all you are, and the day you leave it, you will retrace your steps back to where it found you."

But in his mind the die was evidently cast. The decision had doubtless been secretly made in his mind for some time, but had not before been expressed in words. From that night the elder was not quite the same toward our people and the work at large. He continued as a worker for several years afterward, but was retrograding in power all the time. The feeling that being an Adventist was his principal hindrance increasing as time passed, he finally reached the conclusion that he could achieve his goal of fame through denouncing the unpopular doctrines of the denomination, and he finally worked himself out of the denomination and into his self-imposed task of attempting to "expose" it.

All the years intervening between the time of our Chicago association in 1880, and 1903, I occasionally corresponded with Elder Canright, always attempting to do all in my power to save him from wrecking his life and injuring the cause he had done so much to build up. At times I felt hopeful, but every time my encouragement was smothered in still blacker clouds.

I finally prevailed upon him to attend a general meeting of our workers in Battle Creek in 1903, with the view of meeting many of the old workers and having a heart-to-heart talk together. He was delighted with the reception given him by all the old workers, and greatly pleased with the cordiality of the new workers. All through the meetings he would laugh with his eyes full of tears. The poor man seemed to exist simultaneously in two distinct parts—uncontrollable joy and relentless grief.

Finally when he came to the Review and Herald, office, where I was then working, to tell me good-bye before returning to his home in Grand Rapids, Michigan, we went back in a dark storeroom alone to have a talk, and we spent a long time there in this last personal, heart-to-heart visit. I reminded him of what I had told him years before in Chicago, and he frankly admitted that what I predicted had come to pass, and that he wished the past could be blotted out and that he was back in our work just as he was at the beginning, before any ruinous thoughts of himself had entered his heart.

I tried to get him to say to the workers there assembled just what he had said to me, assuring him that they would be glad to forgive all and to take him back in full confidence. I never heard any one weep and moan in such deep contrition as that once leading light in our message did. It was heart-breaking even to hear him. He said he wished he could come aback to the fold as I suggested, but after long, heartbreaking moans and weeping, he said: "I would be glad to come back, but I can't! It's too late! I am forever gone! Gone!" As he wept on my shoulder, he thanked me for all I had tried to do to save him from that sad hour. He said, "D. W., whatever you do, don't ever fight the message."

This a brief statement of the downfall of one of the leading men in our denominational work, brought about through the gradual development of a germ of self-exaltation.

MY "TALL TIMBER" DAYS

AFTER graduating from Hamill's School of Oratory in Chicago, I returned to Battle Creek and published "Ten Lessons in Elocution" in pamphlet form, forty pages and covers, designed to give in concise form the outlines of the science and art of elocution in ten lessons. It was to be used as a textbook in a short course of study. It was furnished free to all taking lessons. Then I went back home to my old district schoolhouse, and taught ten lessons free of charge to a large class of my former schoolmates.

At the close of the ten lessons we gave an entertainment, in order to demonstrate what improvements could be made in a short course of only ten lessons. All the people in the community turned out, and in the collection taken to cover expenses, ample was given to cover a good salary for the time spent.

At this entertainment I was deluged with invitations to organize classes in neighboring districts at my regular prices; so I was kept busy all winter with class work in the evening and private individual work all day. It was a pleasant and highly remunerative work. But my heart was not in applying what I had gained in this way, and the longer I worked teaching elocution, the more dissatisfied I became, and I was really comforted when, after the diphtheria scourge in which I was caught, I found my

185

voice so changed I could not properly illustrate the different qualities of voice, and could not longer successfully teach the science.

When I again came back to Battle Creek, after giving up teaching elocution, hoping in some way to get into the literature work, there seemed to be no opening. I had to do something, for I was then about twenty-eight years of age, and was planning to be married sometime soon, but I wanted to be established in whatever I was going to do before I was married. The regular canvassing work in the denomination was not then established. We had no subscription books. Years afterward, I bought of George King, our first subscription book canvasser, the first subscription book that the denomination completed. It was after many years given back to the publishers, and is now kept as a relic in the safe of the Art Department of the Renew and Herald publishing house. Doubtless I would have taken up the canvassing work then had there been such a work, for I had sold other publications before I entered Battle Creek College.

I solicited for the *Phrenological Journal,* and sold all of Fowler and Wells' high-priced books. But I did not canvass from house to house as our canvassers do today. I got together groups of people, and explained to them what I had for them, making demonstrations in various ways, and took orders after I finished. Of course there were always those who were interested, but not ready to order then. On all such I called later personally at their homes, but usually managed to have other neighbors present, who had not been present at the former explanation. I worked in the main with groups of people. I had a large-sized model of the perfect phrenological human head, on which I pointed out the location of all the different parts of the human brain, and then gave a demonstration by examining the head of anyone who would volunteer to be examined in public.

Anyone who had some conception of human nature can judge reasonably well of almost everyone's general make-up without feeling of his or her head, but for business purposes, he can find plenty of complimentary things to say about the one examined, that will make him or her feel glad that the examination was so favorable. When the one examined is obviously a tough customer, as was often the case, the examiner knows enough to stress what he is capable of doing, rather than what he really is. This worked for the good of a number of tough fellows, and made those who heard feel better toward them.

Phrenology had quite a popular run back in the 70's. Even after I came to Battle Creek, a phrenologist visited that place and had a hearty reception. He examined heads before a large audiences. He would ask his audience to call on some well-known person to be examined. One night Elder Smith was present, and the students of the college persistently called for him, and he went up and was examined before the large audience. This phrenologist knew his business. He knew the elder was a popular man, from all appearances, and gave him a fine character, with gifts in the superlative degree. I give this instance in proof that phrenology was then popular. Phrenology, however, like many other so-called sciences, is unscientific and not half reliable.

At that time our conferences did not have openings for beginners, and the publishing house did not seem to want me, so I got a job clerking in a combined grocery and bakery store at six dollars a week, six days a week, fifteen hours a day, the lowest salary I ever drew before I spent thousands of dollars going to school. But I would have worked for nothing rather than do nothing. It did not seem to me, however, to be just right, after all I had done, to be thus humbly employed as such a small wage. It was not, however, less than the herding of sheep by Moses after he thought he was ready for his lifework.

While thus employed, I was married. Many of our girls today will wonder why Mrs. Reavis would marry a six-dollar man, when she was a regular public school teacher, drawing a good salary, and had been for sixteen years, and could continue her position as long as she wanted to. Well, it was a wonder to me then, and has been all these years. But she did, and we lived happily together for almost fifty years. She always said she made no mistake.

The fact is, neither of us thought of finances at all. We did not believe time would continue very long. We were never rich, only in contentment, but always had enough for our good. We never went into debt above our ability to pay out easily, even in times of depression. Through close application to business, and economy, any couple can prosper on a single small salary. Mrs. Reavis, after marriage, never worked outside of her home, only to help out for a few days in emergencies, yet we accumulated a little from every job I had, from the first six dollars a week to the last week she lived.

A little less than a year after I entered the grocery store, Mrs. Reavis's brother needed help in his broom factory. All I knew about the broom business was how to grow broomcorn, and how to use a broom after it was made. I had raised broomcorn and baled it for market, but I had never seen a broom made until I saw my brother-in-law make one. I went into the broom factory as an employee for just enough wages to pay for our groceries, until I could learn the business sufficiently to make more by piecework. It was not long before I could make twelve dollars a week on piecework. At that time twelve dollars a week was considered a good salary, but I was wanted to do all kinds of work, including the selling and collecting. One week in every month I spent on the road, selling brooms to merchants in other towns in Michigan and Ohio.

To my line of brooms and brushes, I soon added knit goods made by a Novelty Knitting Company of Battle Creek, and extended my time on the road in the fall and winter.

In those days everybody in Michigan and Ohio wore heavy woolen socks and stockings during the winter season, also heavy knit gloves, mittens, and wristlets. The ladies, when outdoors, wore long, heavy-knit leggings that covered their limbs from the sole of the shoe to six or eight inches above the knee—quite a contrast with the present style of limb exposure.

These knit goods, with brooms during the fall and winter, made a good-paying commercial line, and kept me on the road most of the time during the fall and winter months. So my recent need of a business resulted in making me a traveling salesman and a broom man in every detail, from raising the corn to making and selling the brooms, and even to wearing the brooms out in everyday use.

During the summer season, the knit goods business was dead and the broom business dull; so I had to find something to do during the summer. Having worked under a master house painter who had been thoroughly taught the trade, instead of just picking it up as most painters do today, I went into the painting business, including all house finishing and decorating, which I continued to operate summer and winter until the call came for me to take up the circulation of religious liberty literature under the direction of Elder A. O. Tait, then secretary of the old International Religious Liberty Association.

ENTERING THE LITERATURE WORK

ALL through these years of my "tall timber" experiences, I was longing for an opportunity to engage in the circulation of our literature on a large scale. This was my burning desire during all the time I was apparently wholly absorbed in the things I was doing. While my hands and my time were given to these worldly enterprises, my heart's desire was in our literature work.

Up to the time of the fifth year of my college work, I thought of nothing else except teaching the message through preaching, but during the two seasons I served in tent work I found that the people who read our literature as they attended the meetings, developed faster and were more intelligently and thoroughly established in the third angel's message than were those who did not read. This was so apparent that it made a deep impression on my mind, and I became thoroughly convinced that there was even greater power in the printed page than in the spoken word. This conviction became so strong I resolved to devote all my future efforts to the production and circulation of literature teaching present truth.

I have had a number of impressive object lessons on the power of our literature in connection with my work in different places. In 1891 and 1892 the National Reform Association, with headquarters in Allegheny, Pennsylvania, began a campaign in the State of Michigan for better Sunday observance. Our religious liberty literature was extensively circulated all over the State, and personally placed in the hands of State legislators, county and State officials, and prominent lawyers. This completely thwarted the Reformers.

In this campaign against the Reformers in Michigan the Battle Creek church assumed the responsibility of placing religious liberty literature in every home in Calhoun County. A business meeting of the church was called for the purpose of getting members to volunteer to do this work. Four men agreed to take the responsibility of seeing that the work was done. Two of these did nothing at all. The other two fulfilled their promise to the church, and completed the job, though it took them all winter to do it.

One who has never circularized a county has no conception of the size of the job. I was one of the two who did this work. I was running a business of my own, but I left my work in the hands of an employee, and gave my full time for the entire winter to this important work. My business did not suffer in the least, It gained all through the winter.

We sent the literature by mail to all taxpayers in scattered parts of the county, obtaining the privilege of taking the names and addresses of taxpayers from the county tax records. Mrs. Reavis and I spent more than a week copying these names from county records in the county courthouse. We gave our time and paid our own expenses, boarding in the county seat while we were doing this work, and had a pleasant and enjoyable time. In other places, not reached by mail, I went to the district school-houses, visited the schools in a friendly, entertaining way by giving reading lessons and recitations, thereby getting the good will of the teachers, and pupils, and sending home the packages of literature to the parents by the children, who voluntarily took the literature to the hones of the people who had no children in the school. This was easier, faster, and proved to be just as good as a time-consuming house-to-house delivery.

In the following fall I was employed by the International Religious Liberty Association at nine dollars a week, and was sent to Pittsburgh, Pennsylvania, with a large truckload of religious liberty literature. The National Reformers were at that time having their own way in the enforcement of Sunday laws throughout the State of Pennsylvania. Their headquarters were located in Allegheny, just across the river from Pittsburgh, and they were bearing down heavily upon the employers of the mill workers in Pittsburgh at that particular time.

Not being accustomed to such a rushing manufacturing city as Pittsburgh, and feeling the weight of the responsibility placed upon me to battle a foe as strong as I knew the Reformers in that place to be, I felt intimidated, and was greatly perplexed over the problem of how to begin the work. My first day in Pittsburgh was spent on an unoccupied spot on a high hill overlooking Pittsburgh and Allegheny. The day was as clear as a day could be in Pittsburgh, with clouds of smoke coming from its forest of smokestacks, but I could see through the smoke the hundreds of iron mills and hear their thunderous roar.

All this sight and sound completely overwhelmed me, and I

wept bitterly as I prayed earnestly for strength and power to do the work assigned to me. Everything had seemingly worked against me so far. I was weary and almost discouraged. The journey to Pittsburgh, though not of so many miles, was a long and a very unpleasant one,. The association secured me railroad tickets to Pittsburgh over a little one-train-a-day road by way of Wheeling because it was cheaper. It paid only my fare, and desired to make that as cheap as possible.

We left early in the morning on a freight train, with a passenger coach attached. We took our lunch, expecting to be in wheeling early that afternoon, but we were bumped along until midnight before we reached Wheeling. The State fair was being held there, every hotel was full, and there was no train to Pittsburgh until six o'clock the next morning. One hotel allowed us to sit in its parlor until our train time, but could not give us any warm food or a bed.

Our train left before any eating place was open. There was no dining car on our train between Wheeling and Pittsburgh, and no possible chance to get anything to eat or drink at any station at which stops were made, no newsboy on the train. Simply nothing, was our lot. I could stand it, but Mrs. Reavis was not accustomed to roughing it in this fashion, and she landed in Pittsburgh that afternoon too sick to want anything to eat, almost too sick to walk.

We found our way to an old, dilapidated building used as a mission, our only meeting place in Pittsburgh at that time. We were permitted to stay there that night, but had to sleep on a bed couch with broken-down springs and a regiment of hungry bedbugs. No sleep that night, but the bugs had a feast, and we a very unpleasant time. The hotel parlor the night before was far preferable.

Everything seemed so dirty, Mrs. Reavis's stomach continued to revolt, and she had a hard time of it. It all was depressing, to say the least. We learned later how to travel in comfort, but we paid well for our first experience. It is no wonder my job seemed so stupendous to me under such circumstances, but I took it all to the Lord on the hilltop, and I know He led me in all my efforts there. He gave me plans of procedure that I could not have thought of.

First of all, I interviewed the editors of the daily papers, and found them nettled by the tyranny of the Reformers. I offered to supply them with crisp copy against religious intolerance and the enforcement of Sunday laws. I copied some of our tracts, adapting them to local conditions, and submitted the copy to the editors. They were greatly pleased with them, and printed them as fast as I could supply them. Mrs. Reavis spent most of her time copying these publications according to my adaptation I got our writers to send me many articles for the press.

I also went to the police department, and secured permission to distribute my literature. No one could put out free matter without a permit, and a fee had to be paid for it; but as I had nothing to sell, and the literature was in opposition to the disliked Reformers, I was not charged. Police aid was given me in getting permission to work in the large mills of that manufacturing city and the railway offices and other places I could not have worked without police help.

Then I got most of the few people we had in Pittsburgh at that time to help me, and I hired newsboys as often as my nine dollars a week would allow to climb the many long stairways and entrances to residences. I sowed Pittsburgh and Allegheny with our literature, and dealt the Reformers a blow which was the beginning of the end of their predominating power in that State.

While my literature circulation in Pittsburgh was at its height, I arranged for a mass meeting in the leading theater on a Sunday night. Theaters were permitted to open on Sundays only for religious services. The cost of the theater therefore on Sundays was less than half the usual price. I was sure the collection would be ample to cover the theater charges; so I sent for A. T. Jones and generously advertised his lecture. The newspapers charged me nothing for the advertising, and sign painters furnished free a large and very attractive notice of the lecture to be used in front of the theater.

It rained hard all day on that Sunday, and still harder just before the hour set for the lecture. Very few people were on the streets, but a street car trolley broke right in front of the theater, and made a thrilling display of light. Fire engines came to the scene, and so did thousands of people. The break was soon repaired, and the people, seeing the theater all lighted up and the attractive bulletin boards announcing the subject, soon filled the theater. We had a meeting worthy of all the publicity gladly given by the friendly press of the city. And the people paid all costs. Soon after the Pittsburgh lecture, I made arrangements for A. T. Jones to deliver a theater lecture in Harrisburg.

This was my first effort in the work to which I felt I was called, and in which I felt satisfied. When I was asked to go to Pittsburgh, it was thought by the officers of the Religious Liberty Association that I should go simply for the winter, but I told them I was going to sell my home and take Mrs. Reavis with me, that I was going to cut loose from my worldly entanglements, and go into the work wholeheartedly. They gave me to understand that I was employed for only that one job, nothing further. But I sold out in a few days, at a time when property in Battle Creek was not selling at all, and went to Pittsburgh unentangled from all other cares. I felt no concern for the future.

In the spring of 1893 I was sent through the Southern States as advance agent for a course of public religious liberty lectures by James T. Ringgold, author of "The Legal Sunday," and in the fall of that World Fair year I was sent south to circulate religious liberty literature in connection with the imprisonment of many of our people of Sunday labor. It would require a large volume to recount all the thrilling experiences of the five hard-working years in that field. While they were the richest years of my life in experience, they demanded the hardest work I ever performed. I attended the trials of forty-two of our people during these five years, and got them out of the clutches of Sunday laws through the influence of our literature.

Some of our people involved in these imprisonments brought the trouble unnecessarily upon themselves. To illustrate, I cite the case of one of our canvassers. He felt he was getting the mark of the beast through not working at manual labor on Sundays. He could preach to country churches on every Sunday of the year; the churches wanted him to preach to them on Sunday. He was a good speaker, and he was at liberty to preach on any subject he wanted to.

But in doing this, he felt he was endorsing Sunday rest. So he rented a small piece of land on a public highway, and spent his Sundays in planting and cultivating potatoes. He was arrested for Sunday labor, and the people who knew him would not buy his "Bible Readings." I went to help him in his trouble, and from the prosecuting attorney and the judge of the court that was to try him, I found out the facts, and promised that this offense would not be repeated by this brother if they would let him off. I gave these men and all other officials there just the literature they should have to convince them that Sunday laws were unconstitutional and wrong in every way. Before the trial, these men found some irregularity in the indictment, and threw the case out of court, and no more arrests were made in that place, though some of our people there did do reasonable work on Sunday.

I asked this canvasser why he did not canvass on Sundays, why he did not interest the people in his books through his preaching. To show him how, I took one of his appointments in a country church, and preached a sermon on baptism, using a full leather "Bible Readings" for a Bible, and when through, I explained that all I had told them was taken from that book, and that any of them, with that book, could present that subject and many others, just as well as I could. I made a short canvass and got subscriptions for it right there; I think sixteen full leather bindings were sold at that meeting. That was more than this canvasser was selling in a week.

In another case I stopped at a large cotton farm in cotton-picking time. Cotton was picked by hand in those days. There were no cotton-picking machines then; they came into use later. There were about twenty-five men staying on this farm at that time. In the evening, as I was with twenty-five or more cotton pickers lying on the grass in the yard of this farm a bright star shot across the sky, and the men all saw it and began to talk about it.

I asked them about the great meteoric shower in 1833, and none of them knew about it. So I told them all about it, and explained that it was a fulfillment of a part of Christ's prophecy recorded in Matthew 24 concerning the end of the world, and of other things I had read in a book I could get for them if they would care to have it. I told them the book would cost each of them five dollars, and if the owner of the farm would collect the money and send it to me, I would order the books for them. Ten ordered "Daniel and the Revelation," and the owner of the farm sent me the money upon the arrival of the books. I made this farm my headquarters for about a week, and sent the owner a copy of "Daniel and the Revelation" in payment for my board.

He lent me an old mule to ride in my work of delivering religious liberty literature in that community. That mule was a very clumsy, lazy old fellow. One would have to bestow about as much energy in keeping him moving as was necessary to use in walking. He could move, however, in various ways when he thought moving was to his interest.

One afternoon, about an hour before sunset, I was passing through a strip of timber. A swarm of big black horseflies attacked this mule, and I, with the aid of the flies, whipped him into a fast gallop in order to get through the timber and away from the flies as quickly as possible. As soon as I succeeded in getting him to gallop, he got all his feet tangled up and went tumbling to the ground headfirst, and I was thrown over his head into a shallow puddle of muddy water.

Before I could get up, my mule was up and gone on his way back home at a speed I could not believe it was possible for him to attain. My literature was strapped to the saddle and was therefore carried back home on this riderless mule, and I walked the several miles back to the farm, meditating on mule nature in general.

The cotton pickers had a good prolonged laugh when they saw me. I was a sight. It took me a long time to get cleaned up. Fortunately, my clothes were of light material and could be washed. It would have been interesting and instructive to anyone who was not familiar with mule nature to have heard these cotton pickers opinion of anyone attempting to use a mule as a saddle animal, especially if an attempt were made to acquire a speed greater than a walk. They said, however, that in one thing a mule has more sense than a horse, or even a man: he knows enough to keep quiet when he finds himself all tangled up. Perhaps that was what this mule was attempting to do when he went heels over head, upon finding he feet tangled.

Soon after this experience, one of our brethren living in Tennessee was arrested and lodged in jail for hoeing in his garden on Sunday. I went to see what could be done toward getting him out of jail during the time he had to wait for trial. Having heard something about this brother and his family, I went first to his home. I found he had a small rented place of about ten acres of land which he cultivated at odd times when he was not employed by nearby farmers; that on this land was a shack of a house in which he, his wife, and little four-year-old girl lived.

I found the little pitifully neglected child some distance from the shack down toward the public road, and she was softly crying. I picked her up and asked her where she lived. She pointed to the shack, which, upon inquiry, I had learned was the home of this imprisoned brother. I carried her to the door, which was open, and saw a poorly dressed woman lying on the bed. She was crying too.

I told this pale, sick woman who I was and for what I had come. She broke down completely, and sobbed and cried for a long time before she could speak. Her crying alarmed the child, for she thought I was another bad man who had come to take her mamma away. It had not been many years since I had buried my two little girls about this child's age in one short week, and up to that time the crying of a child would bring me to tears. So all three of us wept together, while I held the little girl to my heart, and under the circumstances thought how blessed my little ones were, compared with the living one I was then holding.

I was never so indignant toward any people as I was toward the people of that neighborhood for allowing this poor sick young mother and almost starved child to be there all alone without anything to eat in the house. No one had come to see them after the sheriff had taken the husband and father away. The prejudice in that neighborhood was worse than heathenism, because it was established in professedly Christian hearts, and was blacker than many a heathen heart could endure.

I went to the farm where this imprisoned brother worked most of the time, introduced myself, and told the farmer in very plain, comprehensive language why I was there. I expressed the indignation provoked by the sinful way this poor man's sick wife and child were being neglected by a community professing to be so religious they could not bear to see a man work on their unscriptural sabbath day.

I was so completely indignant I was boiling over, and actually commanded him to hook up a horse and drive me to the village to get food for this poor woman and child. He said he could take the food from his supply, and I told him to do so at once, while I went to a colored man's house a short distance away to secure a cook. I put a colored cook in this home and left money for her wages. As I stopped in the village on my way to the county seat, where this brother was in jail, I arranged for groceries and other needed things to be sent to this humble home, and for all bills to be sent to me at Atlanta, Georgia.

My general behavior during the few hours I spent in that neighborhood seemed to change the whole atmosphere. That neglected home became the center of attraction, and there was no further neglect or want. This then heartbroken sister wrote me later that she felt like a queen because of the attention and service given her.

I found the arrested brother in a very filthy jail. I learned what his diet consisted of, and that his meals were sent to him from the cheap hotel at which I was staying. I went to the proprietor and explained the case to him., letting him know who I was and why I was there. By paying extra charges myself, I arranged for our brother to have good food. Nothing of this kind could be charged to the Religious Liberty Association. I paid for it myself, and was happy in doing it. I told the brother I had visited his home, and had arranged for his wife and child to be properly cared for; that he need not worry about them, and that now I was going to work for his immediate release; that I would see him every day I was there, to be of good cheer, and to live in constant prayer of release without trial.

I made arrangements for a joint meeting of the judge, prosecuting attorney, and sheriff. That was a most interesting affair, entirely too complicated to report in detail, but I told these very considerate men the situation in which I found the prisoner's family, and what I had done upon the order of the International Religious Liberty Association of New York City; the condition in which I found the prisoner in the jail, how the whole affair appealed to me, and how it would be looked upon by the people everywhere when known.

I cited the character of the party entering the complaint against this humble, inoffensive, conscientious Christian man, the religious nature of the law under which he was indicted, and the unreasonableness of forcing him to stay so long in a filthy jail awaiting trial set so far ahead of the arrest, all for hoeing in his garden on Sunday. It was the same kind of work nearly everybody does more or less on every Sunday during garden time; in fact, the same kind of work the man was doing himself the very day he complained of the prisoner. Then I gave each man a good supply of literature covering the question of Sunday laws and all other religious legislation, and asked them to think the whole matter over carefully, and let me know their decision as soon as possible.

I suggested that the prisoner be immediately release upon the irregularity or technical defect of the indictment, which indictment I had examined. They took me to be a lawyer. They did not ask me, and I did not go to the trouble of telling them I was not.

The next day the prosecuting attorney informed me that upon the advice of the judge, the prisoner would be released inside of forty-eight hours. I went to the jail and told the brother in confidence what the prosecuting attorney told me, bade him goodbye, and took the first train going my way. Before I reached Atlanta, a wire came announcing the brother's release.

TWO MYSTERY MEN

THERE was another case down in the lowlands of Alabama, to which I will refer in order to reveal the bitter spirit associated with and leading up to, this attack upon our people, and to relate an experience through which I passed in connection with this particular case, without recognizing the danger to which I was exposed at the time.

It was the most complicated, bitter case of any of the forty-two with which I was connected because of some very unpleasant and uncomplimentary things charged against the family of the brother being tried for the violation of the Sunday law. The hatred toward our people there was intensified by the flow of moonshine whisky, for whisky was the ruling element in that community.

The courthouse was packed with a mob, brought there to take care of any opposition to the most severe punishment it was possible to inflict upon this despised "Seventh-day Advent." All the court officials were, in my opinion, dominated by the spirit of hatred, produced through the influence of a strong sectarian prejudice. The whole court proceedings in the trial were undignified and pronouncedly sarcastic.

The full penalty of the law was imposed. In some way the

rumor went the rounds that I was there to pay whatever fine was imposed, and they intended to make it as large as possible. When it was found that no fine would be paid, and that the county would have to bear the expense of keeping the prisoner for the long time imposed in case of default in payment of fine, the officials and the mob element were furious. The sheriff, as a matter of bluff, savagely grabbed the prisoner, and led him out some distance from the courthouse to a shack they used for a jail. I went along with them, and the mob followed, in an intensified mob humor.

At the jail door, three or four old Southern army veterans began to plead with the sheriff not to put their old army comrade in jail for only doing a little work on Sunday, a thing they all did every Sunday. They said it was shameful and a disgrace, and they began to cry, and placed themselves in the door, blocking it against the sheriff and his prisoner. The mob began to mill around, demanding that the fine be paid.

Just then a large man forced himself through the crowd and took me by the arm and said, "Come with me." I had no thought of there being any danger whatever so far as I was concerned, and believing the whole affair was practically over, and that this fine-looking man wanted to offer some solution of the situation, I, without hesitation, followed him.

The men of the crowd voluntarily pushed back out of his way. They seemed to be awed by his very presence. Judging from their actions, I thought he was some highly respected man of the community. The only thing he said to me, after clearing the crowd, was, "Let's go back to the courtroom." I supposed he was going there to make me some proposition in connection with the case.

He led the way into the courtroom, taking me well up in front, and as I was adjusting my seat preparatory to sitting down, this mystery man disappeared. He was much larger than any ordinary man, and could easily be seen in an almost empty courtroom, were he there. I thought perhaps I was fussing with my seat longer than I realized, and that he had gone out for something without my seeing him. So I sat down and waited for him. I stayed until court adjourned for the day, some three hours later, but the man did not come back. This greatly perplexed me. I could not understand it.. It never entered my mind that I had been delivered from a dangerous place in a supernatural way, for I knew no fear, and the thought of being in any danger never occurred to me.

The case in which I was interested being disposed of, and there being nothing more I could do, I was ready to leave, but there was no way of getting away before an early hour the next morning. I went to the little hotel, the only one there, for the night. All through that night, the gang of toughs who were there during the day continued their drinking, and kept the little town awake with their yelling, shooting and racing their horses up and down the dirt street in front of the hotel.

The next morning there was quite a busload of people going to the train, more than a half mile outside of the town. The railroad was a lonely spur line, and the county seat was its terminal. The small train was standing on the track when the bus drove up to the station. There another strange man met me and lifted my grip from the bus for me, explaining that I should not lift a bag as heavy as that.

The first night I landed in that damp place I had my first attack of pleurisy, and was able to be around only by being tightly bandaged; but only the doctor and I knew of this, and this man was not the doctor. He carried my grip to the ticket office and into the train, and sat down in the seat with me.

The same rowdies who had been present at the trial the day before were at the station that morning. I wanted to go to the back platform of the car, to see what they were up to, but this man said, "You must stay where you are, for it is damp out there, and you must not expose yourself." The train pulled out and made no stop for forty miles. The road ran that distance through a very swampy section, in which there were no train stops.

Soon after the train started, this man got up and left the car, going toward the smoking car, the only other car comprising the train, it being a combined smoker and baggage car. I wondered if such a fine, clean young man as he really smoked; so I went into the smoker to see what he was doing. He was not there. I went into the baggage end of the car; he was not there. I searched through every part of the smoker and the day coach, but I could not find him. Where could he be? The train had not stopped since we started.

I became so curious I finally asked the conductor what had become of the young man sitting with me when he took up my ticket. He said, "There was no one with you in your seat when I punched your ticket." I declared there was. He as strongly declared there was not. He said, "You must have had an overdose of moonshine."

Well, my experience with the large man at the jail the day before, and now this young-man mystery caused me to think and to wonder, and I am still wondering as I think over the past. I wonder why I did not ask these men more questions; why I was so submissive to all their requests, without knowing more of the reasons for my doing what they requested; why I did not ask them who they were; and many other things I would now like to know definitely. It was all a mystery to me then, and it is to this day.

In a few days the man tried and imprisoned was set free upon the claim that the fine was paid, but I have never found out who paid it, and question whether it was paid at all.

I Remember

MY CLOSING WORK

ONE year, while I was in the South, the General Conference was not able to pay its employees their full salaries, small as they were. They paid as much as they could when the money came in. Mrs. Reavis and I understood the situation, and decided that we would not ask for any money. If the General Conference sent us some without our asking for it, well and good, but we would not ask for it. Six months passed before the secretary of the General Conference asked us what was the matter that we were not asking for money as other workers were.

During that time we were buying our groceries and paying our rent out of our own money. Mrs. Reavis, with her needle and sewing machine, was taking care of our wardrobe. While I was away on a trip, she made over a badly faded suit of mine by turning it inside out and relining it. When I came home, she presented me with a suit as good as new, and then proceeded to do the same with the suit I was wearing. All of my friends thought I had new suits. And we let them think so.

Every little while Mrs. Reavis would come out with a new dress or a new hat made of old dresses and old hats, altered and retrimmed. We appeared to be prospering, and we were, through the handiwork of one who had learned in her youth to make her own clothes, and later acquired ability to do a good tailoring job, which was no more difficult than making a lady's cloak, which she often did. A poor man's greatest aid in life is a wife who can sew and cook.

When we went south, the General Conference was paying only the men's railroad fare, with no sleeper nor freight allowance. If a worker wanted the supposed luxury of a wife, he had to pay her fare and all her expenses. All the five years I was in the South, I was constantly traveling, but I was never allowed a dollar for a sleeper. I sometimes took a sleeper, but I paid for it myself. Many times I worked all day putting out literature, and sat up all night in a day coach, and worked all the next day in order to get the necessary work done before a critical hour. This would seem hard today, but in those days the majority of people were not accustomed to the comforts and luxuries that are common nowadays.

The hot sun and the poisons from ticks, flies, mosquitoes, and bedbugs, so common in the South at that time, undermined my natural vitality, and I became so rundown that it was thought best for me to have a change of climate; so I was ordered to Albany, New York, to work with literature against the Reformers in that State. In so far as my individual good was concerned, this was a bad move, especially since I was leaving the South in the fall. I was chilled through and through all the first winter I was in Albany. It is a wonder I pulled through at all, and I still have the conviction that Albany, New York, is the coldest spot in the United States. Hot and cold applications are good for some afflictions, but I do not recommend them for mere pleasure.

In Albany I found the Reformers as strongly entrenched in government affairs as they were in Pennsylvania, but here I had to battle against the leaders themselves in the capital of the State—in the legislature, instead of against the results of their work in a local city in their territory. The situation was entirely different, and it was necessary to study how best to begin.

I spent some time in becoming familiar with the situation. For several weeks my entire time was spent in the capitol building, listening to the representatives and senators in their discussions, and obtaining a "gallery acquaintance" with as many of them as possible.

At this time the Reformers were bringing heavy pressure to bear upon many members of the State legislature, in an attempt to secure favorable action upon a number of religious bills they had caused to be presented at that session of the legislature. They were coming to the capital from New York City in special cars, as many as fifty or sixty at a time, dressed in their clergy coats and top hats, with valets to wait upon them in every possible way, to make an imposing spectacle of themselves before the legislators, whom they hoped to impress with their dignity, position, and following.

They had a private hall in the capitol building, and they would call the legislators before them, and tell them what they expected them to do about certain pending bills; and when these bills were up for consideration in either the house or the senate, they would be present en masse to see who supported them and who did not. It was all very embarrassing and trying to most of the members of the house and the senate. Many who "toadied" to the Reformers did so in order to get their support "back home" at election time, but they thought less of the Reformers because of their spirit of coercion.

When I found how the majority of the State legislators felt toward the Reformers, I knew how to work with them better than I could have worked without this information. I took advantage of the feeling against the Reformers, and of the course followed by them which created this antagonistic feeling, and proceeded in a way that made the legislators feel everything was in their hands alone—that they were the lawmakers. I made the acquaintance of the doorkeepers of the house and the senate, and through them received much helpful information.

I sent for enough copies of "The Legal Sunday" to supply members of both houses and all other officials connected with the legislature; and through permission of those having charge of the floor of the house and the senate, during sessions, I personally delivered one of these books, with a copy of the *American Sentinel*, to every member and official. A week or so later I personally delivered the copies of "State papers," and finally "The Two Republics" in full morocco bindings. The postmaster in each house allowed me to store my books in his office while I was making my delivery.

It required several days to make these deliveries, because it had to be done when the men were not especially busy, and besides, I wanted to inquire about certain bills and to find out how each legislator regarded them. In this way I became known to all, and they so appreciated the literature I had given them that many came to me for other literature bearing upon some pending reform bill they did not approve. These men appreciated our literature so much that they would invite me to attend some other social functions. I did not always accept these invitations, but some of them I did accept—some of the most informal, where evening clothes were not required.

The literature delivered this first winter so influenced and educated the members of the New York Legislature upon the principles of religious liberty and the evils of religious legislation, that the power of the Reformers began to wane perceptibly; and this work, followed up for three succeeding sessions of the legislature, resulted in an almost complete cessation of reform coercion in that State.

The next year I was sent to New York City to put the pamphlet, "The Legal Sunday," in the office buildings of that city, which had just been made into Greater New York, with a population of 2,000,000. At this time the Pacific Press Publishing Association had a branch office in New York City, in which office the *American Sentinel* was published; and the office of the Religious Liberty Association was located at 49 Bond Street. The headquarters of the Foreign Mission Board was in Philadelphia, but soon afterward was moved to New York City. All of these departments made New York quite a strong center of our work, though there was only one small church in the city of New York and one in Brooklyn.

Elder Allen Moon was president of the Foreign Mission Board, also president of the Religious Liberty Association. His foreign mission work required his presence in Europe that year, and other officers of the Religious Liberty Association were engaged in other responsible positions; so the burden of this department fell upon the secretary of the association, who, being young, became discouraged. Before my literature work was completed, he resigned, and the executive committee of the association appointed me to take his place. This took me out of the field and tied me up in the Religious Liberty office.

At the General Conference held in South Lancaster, Massachusetts, I was elected secretary of the association, and ordered to move the office of the association and the *Sentinel* to Chicago, Illinois, the following spring. When the office was established in Chicago, I resigned, and went back to New York City to complete the work I had left unfinished there. As I was finishing this work, I was called by the Review and Herald Publishing Association to serve a manager of the circulation department, which was to include everything published by that house.

Previous to my taking up work in the Review and Herald, the periodicals and books were separated into two departments. My first work was to unite these and operate then as one department. This combination was maintained for several years after the publishing house was moved to Washington, but the periodicals so rapidly increased in number it was thought best to separate them and the books again. To me was assigned the promotion of the periodicals. Later it was thought best to divide the periodical department by making the magazines *Life and Heath*, *Liberty*, and the *Protestant Magazine* a department by themselves. After a short time the magazines were put back in the periodical departments, where they have remained until the present time.

In 1914 *Present Truth* sprang suddenly into existence, and it grew so rapidly and required so much attention that it was placed in a department by itself; and as I had been persistently advocating such a periodical for the previous fifteen years, and saw in it the possibilities of successfully and economically teaching the message to the masses in connected serial form by the rank and file of our people, and thereby making it possible for all our people to be effective message teachers through its use, I was assigned the circulation of this one periodical, which might appear to some to be a great decline in position and responsibility; but to me it was a decided promotion, for I maintain that one's position in our work, in God's estimation, ranks in proportion to the number of people he is the means of reaching with the message, because teaching the message is the very highest calling in our work. I know *Present Truth* reaches more people outside of our ranks than all the other publications the Review and Herald puts out.

I regard the conception of the plan and the methods of *Present Truth* and its successful establishment in the field as the crowning work of my life. It has been my only ambition all through my life to fulfill, personally, the Lord's requirement of every believer, "Cast they bread [message] upon the waters [people]," and to exercise abiding faith in His promise, "for thou shalt find it after many days." My "bread" has been abundant and constantly vitalizing, and I have humbly devoted my energy to casting it upon the "waters." I have found much of it, and have full faith in finding all of it in the kingdom of heaven.

In the spring of 1909 the executive committee of the General Conference asked the Review and Herald to release me for the work of launching the Harvest Ingathering plan of securing means for the extension of our foreign missionary work. This task I assumed in full confidence of its being a practical way of gathering in money for missions, but it was something new and untried, and the field was not organized for special work.

Many of our workers did not believe in it at first, and were not willing to engage in it. We had only a special issue of the *Review* for our campaign literature, and it was not so skillfully prepared for this kind of work as our literature afterward became. We had no circulars of any kind, and no printed instructions for individual workers. All promotion work had to be done by myself and one stenographer.

It was a herculean task, to be done with little preparation for it, and yet it was the beginning of a work that has proved to be a large source of financial support to our greatly increased mission work from that time to the present. I have always felt it to be a great honor to have been selected to lead out in the promotion of the Harvest Ingathering work.

Before another harvest Ingathering time came, I was transferred back to the department of circulation in the Review and Herald, and remained there, devoting my undivided attention and best efforts until April, 1933, when it was decreed that I should retire, after serving thirty-two years in the Review office and ten years in the field in my chosen work of teaching the message through the circulation of our literature. And while doing this public field and office work, I have constantly served the local churches wherever I have been located for any prolonged time, from janitor to elder, oftentimes serving in several branches of the church work at the same time. In fact, I have always considered my local church work as binding upon me as the work I was paid to do—that it saved me from being a mere hireling.

Made in the USA
Las Vegas, NV
03 January 2022

40182238R00125